MOTIVATOR

In Sync 4

Clare Maxwell

PEARSON
Longman

In Sync 4 Motivator

Authorized adaptation from the United Kingdom edition, entitled *Upbeat*, first edition, published by Pearson Education Limited publishing under its Longman imprint. Copyright © 2009.

American English adaptation, published by Pearson Education, Inc. Copyright © 2011.

Pearson Education, 10 Bank Street, White Plains, NY 10606, USA

Staff credits: The people who made up the *In Sync* team, representing editorial, production, design, and manufacturing, are Margaret Antonini, Danielle Belfiore, Iris Candelaria, Aerin Csigay, Dave Dickey, Ann France, Lisa Ghiozzi, Emily Lippincott, Leslie Patterson, Stella Reilly, Mary Rich, Barbara Sabella, Donna Schaffer, Julie Schmidt, Mairead Stack, Jennifer Stem, Katherine Sullivan, Jane Townsend, Paula Van Ells, Lauren Weidenman, and Adina Zoltan.

Text composition: TSI Graphics
Text font: Helvetica Neue 10/17

ISBN-13: 978-0-13-254832-8
ISBN-10: 0-13-254832-1

PEARSON LONGMAN ON THE **WEB**

Pearsonlongman.com offers online resources for teachers. Access our Companion Websites, our online catalog, and our local offices around the world.

Visit us at **pearsonlongman.com**.

Printed in the United States of America
1 2 3 4 5 6 7 8 9 10—V012—15 14 13 12 11

Photo credits: All original photography by TSI Graphics and Pearson Education Limited/Gareth Boden. Cover Shutterstock.com; Page 10 Marcel Mochet/AFP/Getty Images; p. 20 Jon Arnold Images Ltd./Alamy; p. 21 (top) Jamie McCarthy/Wirelmage/Getty Images, (bottom) Marco Secchi/Alamy; p. 22 (A) Kjell Brynildsen/iStockphoto.com, (B) PCL/Alamy, (C) Gavin Hellier/Robert Harding World Imagery; p. 36 Jon Kopaloff/FilmMagic/Getty Images; p. 40 Central Press/Getty Images; p. 45 (A) ICP/Alamy, (B) Jorvik Viking Centre, (C) Andrew Holt/Alamy; p. 52 Tom King/Alamy; p. 53 (1-3) Thinkstock Royalty-Free; p. 55 (top) Motoring Picture Library/Alamy, (bottom) Motoring Picture Library; p. 60 Digital Vision/Photolibrary.com.

Illustration credits: Pages 6, 17, 25, 41, 47 David Banks; pp. 50, 57, 59 Bojanna Dimitrovski (Advocate Illustration); pp. 2, 5, 12, 44 Bridget Dowty (Graham-Cameron Illustration); p. 58 Martin Goneau (Advocate Illustration); pp. 31, 49 Brett Hudson (Graham-Cameron Illustration); pp. 2, 3, 11, 15, 16, 23, 26, 38, 42, 56 Joanna Kerr; pp. 7, 18, 35, 46; Anita Romeo (Advocate Illustration); pp. 19, 24, 39, 51 David Shenton; pp. 8, 30, 37 Ross Thompson (Graham-Cameron Illustration).

Contents

1A	Shop until you drop	2
1B	Figure it out!	3
1C	The right job	4
1D	Consolidation 1	5
1D	Consolidation 2	6
2A	What happened?	7
2B	Growing up	8
2C	Lucy's vacation blog	9
2D	Consolidation 1	10
2D	Consolidation 2	11
3A	Potato pancakes	12
3B	Odd jobs	13
3C	I'm sorry, but	14
3D	Consolidation 1	15
3D	Consolidation 2	16
4A	The best vacation ever	17
4B	Music matches	18
4C	The dinner party	19
4D	Consolidation 1	20
4D	Consolidation 2	21
5A	Dream vacations in the U.S.	22
5B	Disaster crossword!	23
5C	Camping trip	24
5D	Consolidation 1	25
5D	Consolidation 2	26
6A	Phrasal verbs puzzle	27
6B	If I were you	28
6C	Suffix scramble	29
6D	Consolidation 1	30
6D	Consolidation 2	31
7A	Mixed messages	32
7B	School tricks	33
7C	A-maze-ing relationships	34
7D	Consolidation 1	35
7D	Consolidation 2	36
8A	An evening at the Odeon	37
8B	New life	38
8C	Jimmy's bad week	39
8D	Consolidation 1	40
8D	Consolidation 2	41
9A	What did she have done?	42
9B	Suffixes crossword	43
9C	The birthday present	44
9D	Consolidation 1	45
9D	Consolidation 2	46
10A	An important appointment	47
10B	Modern mysteries	48
10C	The suspect	49
10D	Consolidation 1	50
10D	Consolidation 2	51
11A	Here is the news	52
11B	Have your say!	53
11C	Noun and adjective crossword	54
11D	Consolidation 1	55
11D	Consolidation 2	56
12A	Money, money, money!	57
12B	Pete and Olivia's world trip	58
12C	Congratulations!	59
12D	Consolidation 1	60
12D	Consolidation 2	61
	Teacher's notes and Answer keys	62

1A Shop until you drop

1 Unscramble the anagrams and match them to the pictures. Then write the clothes next to the prices.

1 [g] ttwsahseir   2 [ ] lecefe   3 [ ] tusi   4 [ ] ltbarecse   5 [ ] nadanab   6 [ ] gelsging

7 [ ] agroc stnap   8 [ ] ite   9 [ ] gishtt   10 [ ] plif splof   11 [ ] deahdanb   12 [ ] hghi seleh

a) _____ $18

b) _____ $8.50

c) _____ $2.50

d) _____ $40

e) _____ $35

f) _____ $80

g) *sweatshirt* $25

h) _____ $3.95

i) _____ $17

j) _____ $2.50

k) _____ $13.95

l) _____ $4.99

2 Kirsty, Martha, Mick, and Owen went shopping and bought all of the items above. Read the clues. Write what each person bought in the correct column.

Kirsty	Mick	Martha	Owen
		sweatshirt	

- One of the girls bought a new sweatshirt for when she goes jogging.
- Kirsty and Owen never play sports.
- Kirsty has very long hair, and found something to keep it neat.
- Owen bought something dressy to wear to a friend's wedding on Saturday.
- Mick never wears dressy clothes. He bought some pants.
- Martha bought some shoes for the beach.
- Martha bought Kirsty some jewelry for her birthday next week.
- One of the boys bought a warm shirt to wear when he goes biking.
- Martha returned home with a pair of these to wear to the gym.
- Kirsty bought something to protect her head from the sun.
- One of the boys bought a silk one to wear with his suit.
- Kirsty got a pair of these to wear with the high heels she'd bought earlier.

3 How much did each person spend? Kirsty _____ Mick _____ Martha _____ Owen _____

Figure it out!

1 Write the names of the jobs in the picture frame. Then write the letters in the grid below.

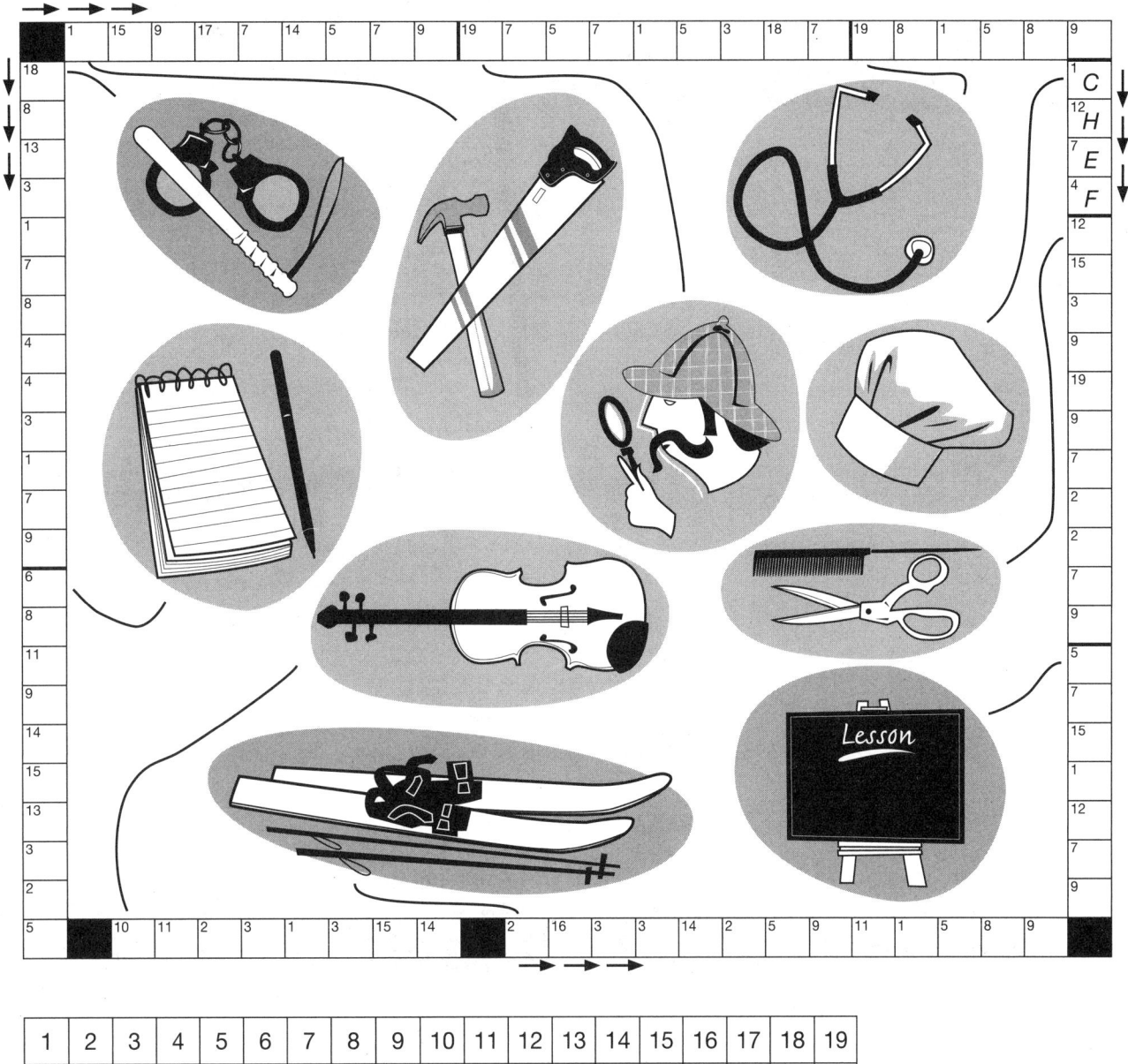

1	2	3	4	5	6	7	8	9	10	11	12	13	14	15	16	17	18	19
C			F			E					H							

2 Use the code in the grid above to work out the famous English proverb.

10	15	14	Y	12	15	14	19	2	10	15	16	7	13	3	G	12	5	W	8	9	16
			Y												G			W			

The right job

1 Unscramble the adjectives in parentheses in the job ads.

Have you ever thought of becoming a reporter?

Are you looking for a more ¹ __glamorous__ (moralugos) job? A job that's never ² _____ (gibron) and uses your excellent writing skills? You have to travel a lot, sometimes to ³ _____ (aegndorus) places. It can be ⁴ _____ (srelstufs) and ⁵ _____ (rignit), but you will meet ⁶ _____ (gneisrtinte) people. And the job is ⁷ _____ (lewl-dipa)! Send your resumé to *jobs@atlantanews.co.us*.

Dynamic teachers wanted!

We are looking for people to join our volunteers in Africa. The job involves working with young people on an ⁸ _____ (uncadetalio) project. This is a ⁹ _____ (witherwhol) opportunity for a qualified person who is looking for a very ¹⁰ _____ (rangweird) job.

Call Matt Smith at 555-679-4242.

Are YOU our new designer?

Are you tired of working in a ¹¹ _____ (luld) office?
Are you ¹² _____ (dylab apid)?
We would like to find a very ¹³ _____ (evarcite) person to do ¹⁴ _____ (gintcixe) work in a busy New York studio. If you have excellent artistic skills and experience with computer design programs, contact us NOW at 800-113-1130!

2 Read Jake's online interview. Which job has he applied for?

▽ | _ ▬ ✕

Where do you live, Jake?
➤ I'm living in Chicago right now. But I'd be happy to move.
And why do you want to leave the job you do now?
➤ Well, it's an office job, which is a little boring. I'd like to travel more.
Have you traveled before?
➤ Yes, I have. I spent a year traveling and working in Asia after I graduated from college.
What did you study in college?
➤ I got a degree in English and took some classes in journalism.
And why do you think you'd be good at this job?
➤ Well, I have perfect qualifications for it. I'm also very good with people . . .
I love meeting people. I met lots of different people on my trip to Asia.
How would you feel about traveling around the world?
➤ That'd be fantastic!

Jake has applied for the job as a _____.

Student A

1 You are the customer. You have $50 and you want to buy these items.
Go to Student B's store and buy what you can.

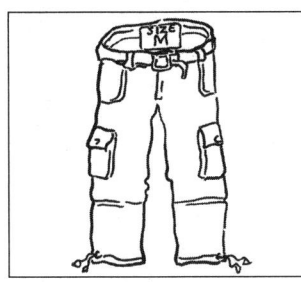   

B: Can I help you?   A: I'm looking for a . . .
B: What size?   A: Do you have it in a . . .? How much is it/are they?

2 You are now the sales clerk. Help Student B buy the things he or she wants.
You have the following items in your store.

- Jeans: sizes S, M, and L $22.50
- T-shirts: all colors, all sizes (but only one in size S) $8

- Sweaters: sizes L and XL $19.50
- Flip flops: sizes 8, 9, 10, and 11 $11

3 Compare with Student B. What did you buy? Who spent the most money?

- -

Student B

1 You are the sales clerk. Help Student A buy the things he or she wants.
You have the following items in your store.

- Cargo pants: sizes S, M, and L $19.50
- Sweatshirts: sizes M and L $15

- Fleece: sizes S, M, and XL $15
- Bandanas: red, blue, green, yellow $2.50

B: Can I help you?   A: I'm looking for a . . .
B: What size?   A: Do you have it in a . . .? How much is it/are they?

2 You are now the customer. You have $50 and you want to buy these items.
Go to Student A's store and buy what you can.

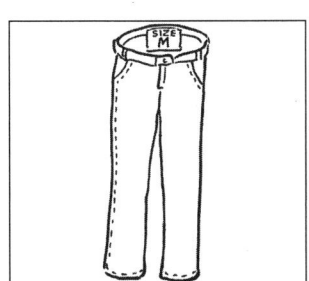 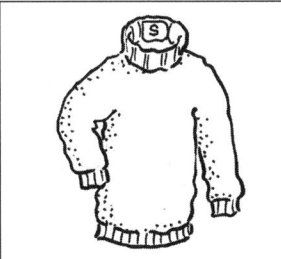 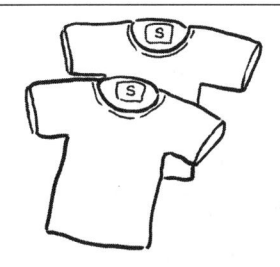 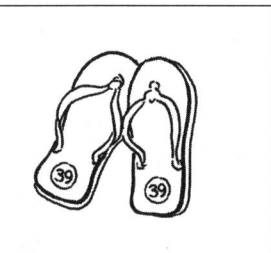

3 Compare with Student A. What did you buy? Who spent the most money?

The train journey

1 Complete the woman's comments with tag questions.

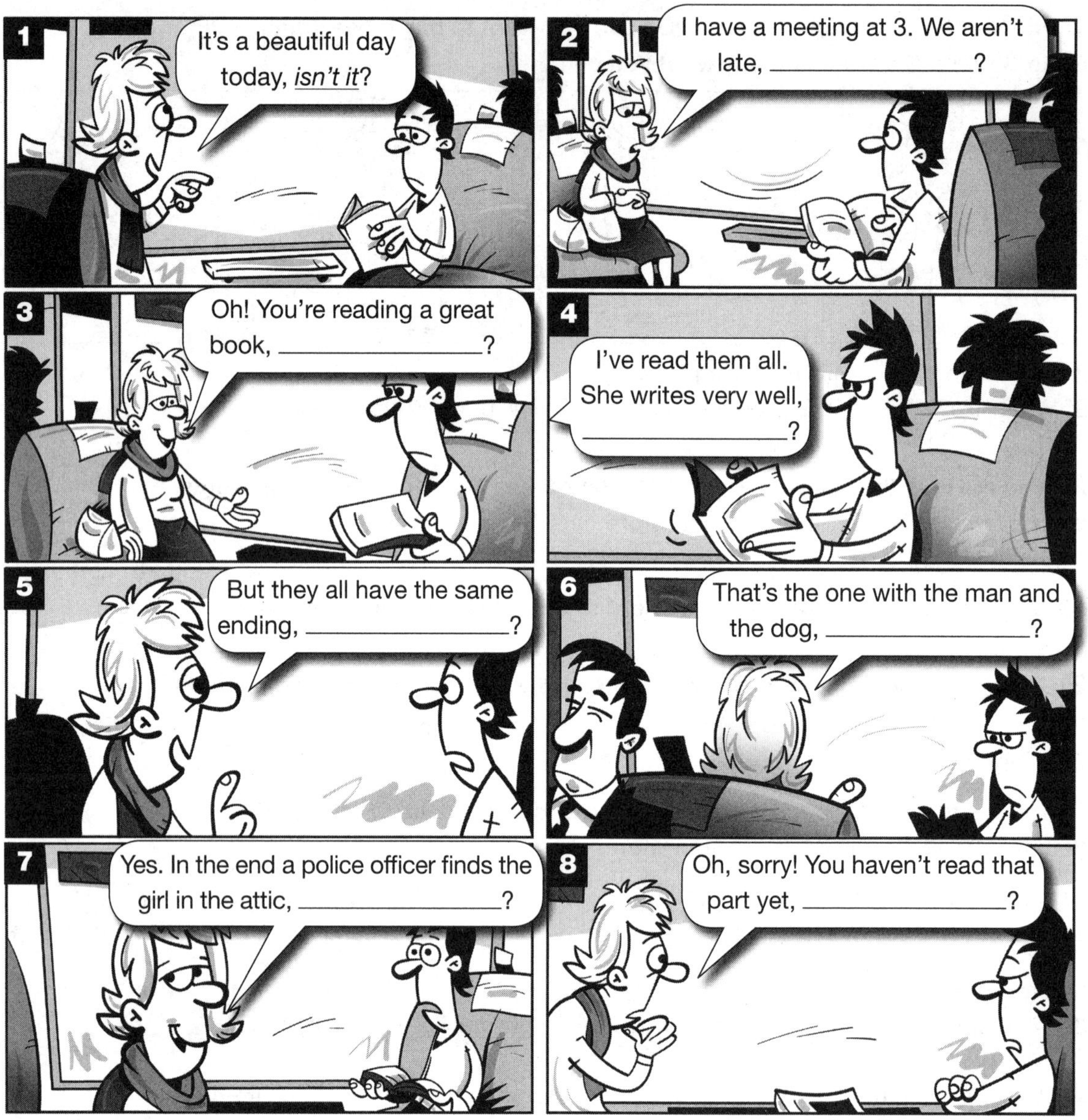

1 It's a beautiful day today, *isn't it*?

2 I have a meeting at 3. We aren't late, _____?

3 Oh! You're reading a great book, _____?

4 I've read them all. She writes very well, _____?

5 But they all have the same ending, _____?

6 That's the one with the man and the dog, _____?

7 Yes. In the end a police officer finds the girl in the attic, _____?

8 Oh, sorry! You haven't read that part yet, _____?

2 Now match the boy's responses to the pictures.

a Um, yes, she does. ☐

b No, I haven't! I'm not going to finish it now. ☐

c Yes, I am. I'm enjoying it. ☐

d Huh? They do? ☐

e What? Oh . . . Yes, it is. Lovely. ☐ *1*

f Um . . . yes, it is. ☐

g Um . . . no, I don't think so. We're on time. ☐

h What?! Don't tell me the ending! ☐

2A What happened?

1 Complete the crossword puzzle with the missing words from the sentences.

(Crossword grid with numbered squares: 1, 2, 3, 4, 5, 6, 7, 8 (h u r t), 9, 10, 11, 12, 13, 14)

Conversation 1

Rick: Lucy, you _hurt_ yourself! What happened? (8 across, 4)

Lucy: Oh, I fell down and broke my arm last week.

Rick: That's too bad! Can I give you a _____ with your bags? (2 across, 4)

Lucy: It's OK, thank you.

Rick: Are you _____? (13 down, 4)

Lucy: Yes, really, I'm _____. (12 across, 4) No _____. (10 across, 7)

Rick: OK, well, I'd _____ get going! See you later! (14 across, 6)

Lucy: Bye, Rick! Thanks!

Conversation 2

Amy: Are you _____? (6 across, 3,5)

Jean: Um . . . yes, I think so . . .

Amy: Did you hurt _____? (1 down, 8)

Jean: No. I'm OK, _____. (9 down, 6)

Amy: Can I do _____ to help? (3 down, 8)

Jean: No, don't _____. (5 down, 5)

Amy: What _____? (4 down, 8)

Jean: I lost my _____ and fell off. (11 down, 7) I'm ok, but I'd _____ some coffee! (7 across, 4)

2 Write the letters from the highlighted squares in the boxes below. Then unscramble the letters to complete the English proverb.

| r | | | | | | | | | | | | |

__ __ __ __ __ __ __ speak louder than __ __ __ __ __.

Growing up

Match the conversations to the pictures. Then complete the sentences with the correct form of the phrasal verbs from the box.

| get up | grow up | hurry up | look up | pick up | stand up | take up | ~~wake up~~ |

a **Alex:** Mom, what are you doing today?
Mom: I've decided to _____ judo . . . I have a class at 10. Now, GO TO SCHOOL!
Alex: OK. Bye, Mom.

b **Mom:** Johnny! *Wake up*! It's seven o'clock.

c **Mom:** Oh, what a mess! _____ those clothes before you go, please.
Alex: Sigh . . . yes, Mom.

d **Mom:** Alex! _____! It's quarter past seven!
Alex: OK, OK . . .

e **Mom:** When will they _____?

f **Johnny:** What's for breakfast?
Mom: Johnny, _____! You're going to be late for school!

g **Alex:** Mom, can you _____ the times of that movie tonight?
Mom: Tonight? But what about your homework?

h **Mom:** Now, where's the paper? Oh, Alex, you're sitting on it! _____!
Alex: Sorry.

2c Lucy's vacation blog

1 Complete Lucy's blog entry with the correct form of the verbs in parentheses. Use the simple past or the past perfect.

Posted at 12:30, Monday, July 23rd

What a journey!

My aunt arrived at our house at 6:30 A.M. yesterday to drive us to Sea-Tac airport in Seattle. We ¹ _got_ (get) in her car and she ² _____ (start) driving toward the airport. I thought, "This is great! This afternoon I'll be in Hawaii!" How wrong could I be? Two minutes later, Dad shouted, "Stop!" He realized that he ³ _____ (forgot) his wallet. So we had to go home again. Of course, by the time we got to the airport, we ⁴ _____ (miss) the flight! There wasn't another flight to Hawaii that day, but Dad ⁵ _____ (call) the airline. They told him that there was a flight from Portland airport at 6 P.M. Portland ⁶ _____ (be) 140 miles away! So we ⁷ _____ (find) a taxi stand and ⁸ _____ (ask) the taxi driver to take us to the train station in downtown Seattle as quickly as possible. There, we ⁹ _____ (get) on a train to Portland. By 3 P.M., we ¹⁰ _____ (arrive) in downtown Portland. Then we ¹¹ _____ (take) the tram to the Portland airport. The ride to the airport lasted 45 minutes. After we ¹² _____ (check) our bags, we had just enough time to find our gate and get on the plane. I was exhausted! I was already asleep before the plane ¹³ _____ (leave) the airport!

---

2 How does Lucy get from Seattle to Hawaii? Number the forms of transportation in the order in which Lucy uses them in her blog.

_____ airplane

___1___ car

_____ taxi

_____ train

_____ tram

Student A

Use the cues to ask Student B questions to complete the article. Follow the order of the numbers.

Ellen MacArthur – Born to sail

In 1980, Ellen MacArthur was [1] ___four___ (*how old?*) years old, and she went sailing with her aunt. After this first sailing trip, she [3]_____ (*what/do?*), and in 1988 she bought a small sail boat. Ellen had alwss wanted to be [5]_____ (*what?*), but she changed her mind when she saw an around-the-world sailing race on TV.

When she was 24, Ellen took part in the Vendée Globe solo around-the-world race. After facing storms and icy seas, she finally arrived in France on [7]_____ (*when?*). She came in second in the race, and took only [9]_____ (*how long?*). She had become the youngest person ever to complete the race. Soon after, in 2005, Ellen broke the world record for the fastest ever solo sailing trip around the world.

When she isn't racing, Ellen gives a lot of time to [11]_____ (*what?*), which she set up in 2003. The trust takes young people sailing to help them recover from serious illness.

✂ ---

Student B

Use the cues to ask Student A questions to complete the article. Follow the order of the numbers.

Ellen MacArthur – Born to sail

In 1980, Ellen MacArthur was four years old, and she went sailing with [2] ___her aunt___ (*who?*). After this sailing trip, she saved her allowance, and in 1988 she bought a small [4]_____ (*what?*). Ellen had always wanted to be a vet, but she changed her mind when she saw an around-the-world sailing race on TV.

When she was [6]_____ (*how old?*), Ellen took part in the Vendée Globe solo around-the-world race. After facing storms and icy seas, she finally arrived in France, on February 11, 2001. She came in [8]_____ (*what position?*) in the race, and took only 94 days. She had become the youngest person ever to complete the race. Soon after, in [10]_____ (*when?*), Ellen broke the world record for the fastest ever solo sailing trip around the world.

When she isn't racing, Ellen gives a lot of time to the Ellen MacArthur Trust, which she set up in 2003. The trust [12]_____ (*what/do?*) to help them recover from serious illness.

Motivator quiz: transportation

Do you like traveling? Or do you prefer to stay at home? Take our quiz and find out!

1 What color are the taxis in New York?

   a) black   **b)** white   **c)** yellow

2 What is a "barge"?

   a) a type of airplane   **b)** a type of bicycle   **c)** a type of boat

3 What is a tandem?

   a) a type of motorcycle   **b)** a minibus

   c) a type of bicycle

4 How many flights take off from London Heathrow Airport every day?

   a) less than 1,000   **b)** between 1,000 and 2,000   **c)** more than 2,000

5 When was the train invented?

   a) in the 18th century   **b)** in the 19th century   **c)** in the 20th century

6 What is one of the actor John Travolta's favorite hobbies?

   a) flying airplanes   **b)** racing cars   **c)** racing speedboats

7 What type of car does James Bond drive?

   a) Maserati   **b)** Porsche   **c)** Aston Martin

8 Which of the following travels the fastest?

   a) the world's fastest helicopter   **b)** the world's fastest train

   c) the world's fastest boat

9 Where did the famous train The Orient Express go?

   a) Amsterdam to Venice   **b)** London to Kiev   **c)** Paris to Istanbul

10 What is Air Force One?

   a) Queen Elizabeth's private plane

   b) the official airplane of the U.S. president

   c) the biggest military plane in the world

My score: _____

8–10	You are an adventurer. You have a great interest in all aspects of transportation.
4–7	You don't travel very often. You only travel for practical reasons.
0–3	You love to stay at home. You aren't really interested in transportation.

3A Potato pancakes

1 Circle the word that doesn't belong in each group of words.

1 (spoon)	peeler	sieve	saucepan
2 bowl	knife	spoon	fork
3 bean	salt	lettuce	tomato
4 lamb	chicken	beef	eggs
5 saucer	cup	frying pan	plate

2 Use the words you circled in Exercise 1 to complete the recipe.

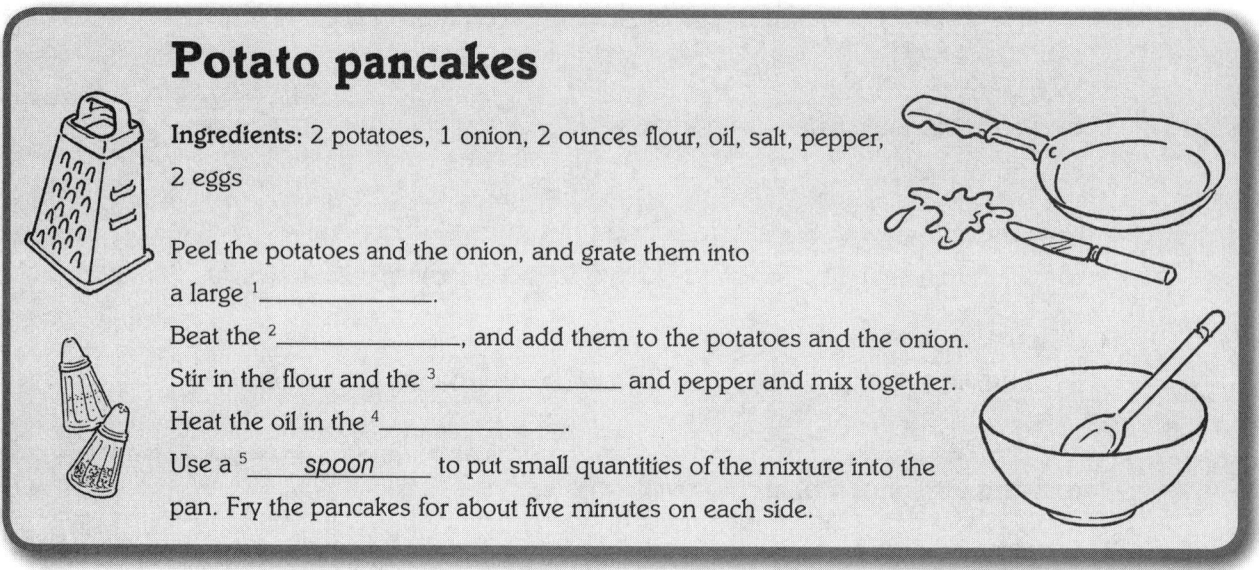

Potato pancakes

Ingredients: 2 potatoes, 1 onion, 2 ounces flour, oil, salt, pepper, 2 eggs

Peel the potatoes and the onion, and grate them into a large ¹_____.

Beat the ²_____, and add them to the potatoes and the onion.

Stir in the flour and the ³_____ and pepper and mix together.

Heat the oil in the ⁴_____.

Use a ⁵____ *spoon* ____ to put small quantities of the mixture into the pan. Fry the pancakes for about five minutes on each side.

3 Jo is buying the ingredients for some fillings for her pancakes. Match the items in her basket with the items on the shopping list. Which ingredient has she forgotten?

SHOPPING LIST

sour cream	b
mushrooms	
salmon	
shrimp	
1 red pepper	
cheese	
2 lemons	

Jo has forgotten the _____.

3B Odd jobs

1 Trace a route through the grid to find nine part-time jobs. You do not need to use all the words in the grid.

START ▶	dog	washing	cars	helping	in
people	walking ▼	store	pets	yard	a
computer	teaching	a	in	money	retirement
skills	jobs	having	working	friendly	home
mowing	lawns	on	newspapers	meeting	baby
helping	weeding	yards	delivering	FINISH! ◀	sitting

1 _____dog walking_____   6 _____

2 _____   7 _____

3 _____   8 _____

4 _____   9 _____

5 _____

2 Use the remaining eight words from the grid to complete the job ad.

Do you have free time ¹_____ the weekends? Do you enjoy
²_____ ³_____? Are you ⁴_____?
Now you can earn ⁵_____ while you are ⁶_____ fun!

Join the Community Help Team!

We do small ⁷_____ for local people: ⁸_____
around the house and in the ⁹_____, and taking care of
¹⁰_____.

Email us at: *oddjobs@highworthcht.org*

3c I'm sorry, but . . .

Student A

1 Look at the three picture cues. Invite Student B to go to these events with you. Student B is busy – can you persuade him or her?

A: Do you want to . . . / Can you . . . / Would you like to . . .?
B: I'd like to, but . . . / I'm really sorry, but . . . / I have to . . .

2 Student B will invite you to go to three events. You have other plans, so you have to give an excuse for each. Choose excuses from the suggestions below, or make up your own. Agree to go to at least one event.

have doctor's appointment	go to Aunt Hilda's birthday	wash the dog
clean Dad's car	watch favorite TV show	study for math test

Student B

1 Student A will invite you to go to three events. You have other plans, so you have to give an excuse for each. Choose excuses from the suggestions below, or make up your own. Agree to go to at least one event.

paint bedroom	make birthday cake for sister	take care of sick cat
don't have any money	visit Grandma in hospital	go to football practice

A: Do you want to . . . / Can you . . . / Would you like to . . .?
B: I'd like to, but . . . / I'm really sorry, but . . . / I have to . . .

2 Look at the three picture cues. Invite Student A to go to these events with you. Student A is busy – can you persuade him or her?

1 Read the problems from the Teen Forum, and complete them using *make*, *let*, or *allowed to*.

TeenTalk

1

Help, please!

Can anyone give me some advice? I'm 16, and I really want to go to the Seattle Pop Festival next month. The problem is that my parents [1] __won't let me__ go! My brother's 18, and he [2] _____ go, and all my friends are going. What can I do?

Janine, Seattle

2

Upset!

Help! Does anyone else have this problem? I live with my mom and my little brother (he's 12). I [3] _____ go out during the week because my mom [4] _____ take care of my brother every evening while she's at work. She only [5] _____ see my friends on Saturday afternoons. I'm 15.

Mick, Des Moines

3

What can I do?

Marina is one of my best friends, but I hardly ever see her out of school. Her parents are very strict, and they [6] _____ meet me after school. They [7] _____ study every evening for four hours, and she [8] _____ go out on the weekends. My parents are the opposite. They [9] _____ see my friends when I want.

Anna, 17

2 Read the replies, and match them to the problems. Each problem has two replies.

a) You shouldn't get involved. It's not your business. [3]

b) You should sneak out and go anyway! They can't stop you! [ ]

c) You should talk to her about it, and tell her you've had enough. [ ]

d) She should take care of your brother, not you! You should go out and enjoy yourself! [ ]

e) I think they're right. Parents should make their children study. It's important for their future. [ ]

f) You should ask your brother to talk to your parents. Maybe he can persuade them. [ ]

Consolidation 2 | *Who does what?*

Six friends have part-time jobs. Read the clues and complete the chart with check marks (✓) and crosses (✗) to help you to figure out who does which job.

- Neither Ben nor Dan need any special skills for their jobs.
- Ellie and Marta both work outdoors.
- Cassie never works on school days.
- Dan is allergic to animals.
- Alec works just two evenings a week.
- None of the girls has to get up early in the morning.
- Alec usually goes to people's houses to do his job, but sometimes they come to him.
- Ben gets up early every morning and bikes a lot for his job.
- Marta can't do her job when it's raining. She works more during the summer.
- Cassie learned her skill from her dad, who builds houses.
- Dan likes his job because he likes taking care of people.
- Ellie often goes to the park to do her job.

	Alec	Ben	Cassie	Dan	Ellie	Marta
Teaching computer skills		✗		✗		
Painting and decorating		✗		✗		
Delivering daily newspapers						
Dog walking						
Mowing lawns						
Helping in a retirement home						

Now write the correct name under each picture.

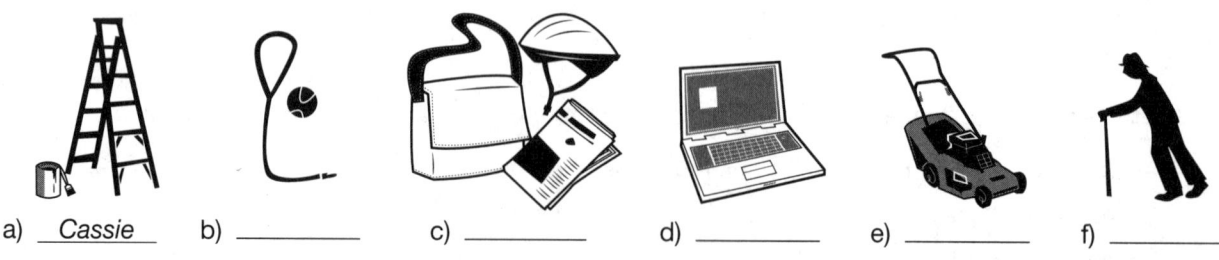

a) *Cassie*   b) _____   c) _____   d) _____   e) _____   f) _____

4A The best vacation ever

1 Complete the sentences with the superlative and present perfect forms of the adjectives and verbs in parentheses. Then match the sentences to the pictures.

a) I just came back from the ___*best*___ (good) vacation I _*'ve ever had*___ (ever have)!

b) We traveled first class on the _____ (comfortable) flight
I _____ (ever be) on!

c) We stayed in the _____ (expensive) hotel on the island.

d) The hotel had its own beach. It was the _____ (white) and
_____ (sandy) of all the beaches on the island.

e) I tried some of the _____ (exciting) water sports you can imagine.

f) . . . and you won't believe it, but I fought the _____ (dangerous)
shark they _____ (ever see) in that area!

2 Make up the end of the story.

Oh, hello, Nick! Has Ben told you about his vacation with his Aunt May in Indiana? She said it was
_____ she
_____!

4B Music matches

1 Aidan is reading his favorite magazine, *MyMusic*. Unscramble the anagrams to complete the excerpts from the magazine. Some of the words have an extra letter.

Disappointing release from LazerEdge

The long-awaited second ¹ _____album_____ (~~ubmal~~) from LazerEdge, *Going to Ground*, has disappointed many fans. The ² _____ (danbs) from Glasgow has good ³ _____ (gnsotserwire), but some of their songs are ruined by two very bad ⁴ _____ _____ (puckab gresins), and the appearance of guest ⁵ _____ (prepara) JayZee T hasn't helped.

Very ordinary. Rating: ✱

WANTED

Punk rock band in London is looking for a
⁶ _____ (bdale resign)
Must have a creative ability to write interesting
⁷ _____ (scorily) for new ⁸ _____ (unsogs)

Contact us at *spiderweb@gtmail.co*

WESTWORLD TOUR CANCELED

Westworld has canceled their tour following the arrest of drummer Mick Allen outside a Chicago nightclub last week. The reasons for his arrest are still not clear.

Westworld shot to fame two years ago when their ⁹ _____ (gellins) "Mix Up" was top of the ¹⁰ _____ (starch) for 16 weeks. Allen has a key role in providing the band's unusual ¹¹ _____ (tabeb). Reports say that Westworld's ¹² _____ (cropedurs) is going to decide whether to end their contract.

2 Write the extra letters in the box. Reorder them to find out what instrument Aidan plays.

d

_ _ _ _ _ _ _

The dinner party

1 **Six friends (three men and three women) are at a dinner party. Read the clues, and complete the information in the chart.**

> **Jobs:** two movie stars, a musician, an artist, an opera singer, a doctor
>
> **Cities:** Moscow, Rio de Janeiro, Rome, London, Lima, New York

	Job	City
Ross	*movie star*	
Marina		
Kate		
Andreas		
Leo		
Carla		

- Ross, who is sitting between a man on his right and a woman on his left, has acted in 20 movies.
- Leo has never visited London. It is the home city of the man opposite him.
- Carla, who is sitting on Leo's right, lives in Italy.
- The doctor, whose name is Kate, is from New York.
- Marina, who met Andreas when he sang in her hometown of Moscow, is sitting between the two movie stars.
- The opera singer, who is very popular in Russia, now lives in Rio de Janeiro.
- The person who lives in New York is sitting between Leo and Andreas.
- Leo, who is secretly in love with Kate on his left, has a movie star from Rome on his right.
- The musician, who is from Lima, is sitting to the left of Carla.
- Ross, who has the same job as Carla, saw the American guest putting a strange liquid into the glass of the person on her left.

2 **Who is sitting where? Write the names of the guests on the table plan.**

1 _____ 2 _____

5 _____Ross_____ 6 _____

3 _____ 4 _____

3 **During the dinner one of the guests was poisoned! Read the clues again and write the names.**

The murderer _____ The victim _____

The witness _____

Consolidation 1 | Good news, bad news

1 Complete the lines of Will and Jade's conversation, and match
Jade's answers to what Will says to make the full conversation.

Will

1 Hi, Jade! I haven't seen you in a __long__ time! How are things? [c]

2 Really? That's cool! Was it fun? ☐

3 Why? What _____? ☐

4 Every day? That's too _____! ☐

5 That's _____. What made you sick? Was it the food? ☐

6 Oh, no! That's terrible! What about the hotel? ☐

7 Oh, Jade, I'm really sorry to hear that. But _____ up! I'm having a party tomorrow! ☐

8 No, I just passed all my classes! ☐

9 Well, I haven't decided yet. But I've organized the biggest party ever! ☐

Jade

a) It was the noisiest place we've _____ stayed in! I haven't slept for days!

b) Well, first it rained every day.

c) Hi, Will. Not bad, thanks. I just got back from a vacation with Mom and Dad.

d) Yeah. It was the wettest weather I've ever seen. And I was sick for three days.

e) Really? Is it your birthday?

f) Hmm, not really. In fact, it was the worst vacation I've ever had. It was _____!

g) _____ job! See you tomorrow, then!

h) Yeah, I think it was probably the worst food I've ever eaten.

i) Wow! _____ great! Are you going to go to college now?

2 Write the answers from Exercise 1 into the grid. Look at the tinted boxes and discover
where Jade went on vacation.

Stars from North America

Student A

1 Read the article about Avril Lavigne, and fill in the information in the box.

Avril Lavigne was born in Ontario, Canada, in September 1984. She has been performing since she was 14 years old, when she sang with Shania Twain at a concert. She released her first album in 2002, and since then she has sold more than 20 million records. In 2002, Avril started acting and starred in the film *Over the Hedge*. Since then she has acted in eight films.

	Avril Lavigne	Justin Bieber
When/born?	September 1984	
Where/born?		
How long/perform?		
When/release/first album?		
How many records/sell?		
How long/act?		

2 Ask Student B questions about Justin Bieber, and fill in the information in the box. Then answer Student B's questions about Avril Lavigne.

3 Compare the information. What do the two singers have in common?

- -

Student B

1 Read the article about Justin Bieber, and fill in the information in the box.

Justin Bieber was born in Ontario, Canada, in March 1994. As a child, he taught himself how to play the guitar, piano, trumpet, and drums, and he has been performing since he was 12 years old. He released his first album in 2009, when he was only 15 years old, and quickly became famous around the world. Since then, his albums have sold several million copies. He is also an actor. In 2010, he appeared in several episodes of the popular TV show *CSI: Crime Scene Investigation*.

	Avril Lavigne	Justin Bieber
When/born?		March 1994
Where/born?		
How long/perform?		
When/release/first album?		
How many records/sell?		
How long/act?		

2 Answer Student A's questions about Justin Bieber. Then ask Student A questions about Avril Lavigne, and fill in the information in the box.

3 Compare the information. What do the two singers have in common?

5A Dream vacations in the U.S.

1 Complete the vacation advertisements.

A

New York City Breaks

Enjoy five days on the east [1] c _o_ _a_ _s_ _t_ in the city that never sleeps! Includes an unforgettable three-hour cruise on the Hudson [2] R _ _ _ _ _ around Manhattan. See the Statue of Liberty and the Brooklyn Bridge, and watch the cruise ships come in at New York [3] h _ _ _ _ _ _! Shopping, museums, and Central Park: there's something for everyone in the Big Apple!

B

California Dreaming . . . and more!

A tour that takes you to three of America's favorite cities! Admire the spectacular [4] c _ _ _ _ _ _ _ _ _ as you drive high up on the [5] c _ _ _ _ _ s along famous Highway 101 from San Francisco to Los Angeles. Swim in the [6] o _ _ _ _ _, and enjoy the beaches in Santa Monica. Then drive east across the [7] d _ _ _ _ _ _ to the bright lights of Las Vegas!

C

National Park Experience

Enjoy the spectacular scenery of Yosemite National Park. Hike in the [8] m _ _ _ _ _ _ _ _ s, and visit some of the highest [9] w _ _ _ _ _ _ _ _ _ _ s in the U.S. and some of the biggest trees in the world! For a completely different experience, take a trip to a very different park in Death [10] V _ _ _ _ _ _, or travel up to Tahoe, where you can visit one of California's most beautiful [11] l _ _ _ _ s and go hiking or biking in the nearby [12] f _ _ _ _ _ _. Your chance to get back to nature!

2 Read the descriptions and match the people to their ideal vacation.

- **Jessica and Susie** are best friends. They love being active, even when they are on vacation. They always do a lot of sports, and particularly like swimming and hiking. They live in a busy city and would like to spend some time in the countryside.

- **Bill and Zoe** are getting married and would like to go the U.S. for their honeymoon. They would like an exciting location. They like city life and love going out to restaurants and theaters. They want to do some sightseeing, but they only have one week for their vacation.

- **Reynaldo and Lucia** have three weeks for their vacation. They have busy jobs, so they would like to be able to relax for some of the time. Lucia loves sunbathing and Reynaldo would like to go sightseeing. Reynaldo is looking forward to trying one of those big American cars!

Jessica and Susie _____   Bill and Zoe _____   Reynaldo and Lucia _____

5B Disaster crossword!

1 Read the clues and complete the crossword puzzle.

Across

3 A tropical storm with high winds (9)
6 Heavy rain, with thunder and lightning (5)
7 Icy rain (4)
9 Sudden, heavy rainfall (8)
12  (8,8)
14 When earth moves down a hill or mountain, usually after rain. (9)
15 The noise that comes after lightning (7)

Down

1 When a lot of snow slides down a mountain (9)
2 A situation when there is no food for people (6)
3 A long period of very hot weather (8)
4 A long period without rain, so plants cannot grow (7)
5 When the earth moves and causes buildings to fall down (10)
8  (7)
10 A very big wave in the sea (7)
11 A snowstorm with strong winds (8)
13 When the water from a river or the sea covers the land (5)

2 Write the letters from the highlighted squares in the boxes below.
Then unscramble the letters to find the name of a volcano in Italy.

 v

5c Camping trip

Student A

Take turns with Student B to ask questions and find eight differences in his or her picture.
Write a number on the picture, and write the difference in your notebook.

Differences: Student B's picture

1 *In my picture the compass is on the table. In Student B's picture it's . . .*

Useful language

Is there a/an . . . in your picture?   Are there any . . .?
How many . . . are there?   Where is it?/Where are they?
On/next to/under/near/behind, etc.

✂ ---

Student B

Take turns with Student A to ask questions and find eight differences in his or her picture.
Write a number on the picture, and write the difference in your notebook.

Differences: Student A's picture

1 *In my picture the compass is under the table, next to the camping stove. In Students A's picture it's . . .*

Useful language

Is there a/an . . . in your picture?   Are there any . . .?
How many . . . are there?   Where is it?/Where are they?
On/next to/under/near/behind, etc.

1 Complete the requests with words from the box.

| buy/that DVD | take me/home | fix/this computer | ~~lend/cell phone~~ |

1 **Emily:** Nick, do you think *you could lend me your cell phone*? I need to call Susie.
   Nick: Sure. Here you are.
   Emily: Thank you. That's really nice of you.

2 **Emily:** Nick, would you mind _____ _____ for me? It isn't working.
   Nick: Of course not. No problem.
   Emily: Thanks, that's great.

3 **Emily:** Nick, could you _____?
   My favorite TV show starts in 15 minutes.
   Nick: Um . . . yes, of course.
   Emily: Thanks a lot.

4 **Emily:** Nick, could you _____ for me? I don't have any money.
   Nick: Um . . . well . . . OK.
   Emily: Thanks! Bye!

2 Put the pictures in the correct order to match the conversations.

3 Complete Emily's final request and Nick's answer.

Emily: Nick, would you mind _____
_____?

Nick: Sorry, I can't. I _____
_____!

Circle the correct answers. Check your answers and write your score.

1 Which country in the world has the longest coastline?
   a) China   **b)** Australia   **c)** Canada

2 What is a "twister"?
   a) a tornado   **b)** a gale   **c)** a hurricane

3 What natural disaster hit an island in Indonesia on December 26th, 2004?
   a) an earthquake   **b)** an avalanche   **c)** a tsunami

4 What is Ben Nevis?
   a) Britain's highest mountain   **b)** an island in the English Channel
   c) the highest waterfall in Wales

5 Which is the most active volcano in Europe?
   a) the island of Santorini in Greece   **b)** Mount Etna in Italy   **c)** Mount Hekla in Iceland

6 Which is the largest desert in the world?
   a) the Gobi   **b)** the Sahara   **c)** the Kalahari

7 What natural disaster occurred in Pompeii, Italy, in 79 AD?
   a) an earthquake   **b)** a landslide   **c)** a volcanic eruption

8 Which country in Europe has the most lakes?
   a) Italy   **b)** Poland   **c)** Slovenia

9 What was Katrina? (Clue: she hit New Orleans in 2005)
   a) an earthquake   **b)** a hurricane   **c)** a tornado

10 Which is the longest river in the world?
   a) the Amazon   **b)** the Nile   **c)** the Volga

My score: _____

8–10	Wow! You're a geography expert.
4–7	Your geography knowledge is pretty good.
0–3	You don't know much about geography!

Phrasal verbs puzzle

Complete the sentences with phrasal verbs from the puzzle.
The correct combinations are always next to each other.

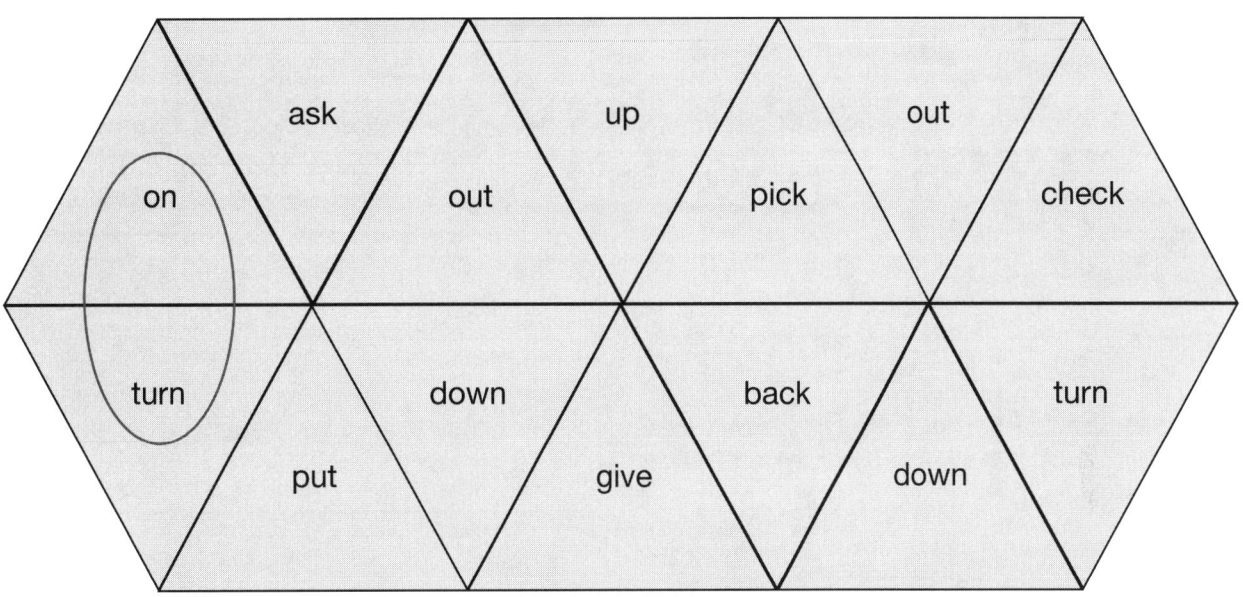

1 It's very dark in here. Why don't you _____*turn*_____ _____*on*_____ the light?

2 This is the police! Don't move and _____ _____ the gun!

3 That music is too LOUD! Will you please _____ it _____?

4 Johnny! Your room is a mess! Please _____ _____ your clothes from the floor and put them away.

5 Jack really likes Chloe. I think he might _____ her _____ soon.

6 Are you free later? I'd really like to _____ _____ that new pizza place in town.

7 Thanks so much for lending me your history notes. I'll _____ them _____ next week, I promise.

6B If I were you...

1 Anna's letter to Isa has been torn up by mistake. Number the pieces in order. Then write the letter in the space povided.

Dear Isa,
Thanks for

hear from you.
Sorry

1 Friday, May 8

call her. Why don't you

to hear about your problems with Tracy. Have you

invite her out for a burger and soda? Anyway, I

were you, I'd wait a few days and then I'd

to study for my geography test. Say

hello to your sister. With love

your letter. It arrived this

from Anna

morning. It was great to

have to go now. I have

tried talking to her? If I

Friday, May 8

2 Answer the questions about the letter.

1 What day did Anna receive Isa's letter? [1 F] [9] [8] [12] [ ] [ ]

2 Who has Isa had problems with? [10] [ ] [ ] [ ] [14]

3 What does Anna think Isa should invite someone out for?
[7] [ ] [ ] [ ] [ ] [ ] and [ ] [2] [ ] [ ]

4 What is Anna studying for? [4] [ ] [5] [ ] [3] [13] [ ] [11] [ ]   [6] [ ] [ ] [ ]

3 Write the highlighted letters from Exercise 2 in the correct squares below. (Use the numbers in the boxes to help you.) What problem does Isa have with Stacey?

Isa [1 F] [2] [3] [4] [5] [6]   Tracy's [7] [8] [9] [10] [11] [12] [13] [14]

Suffix scramble

1 Complete the sentences with the correct nouns. Then write the nouns in the boxes.

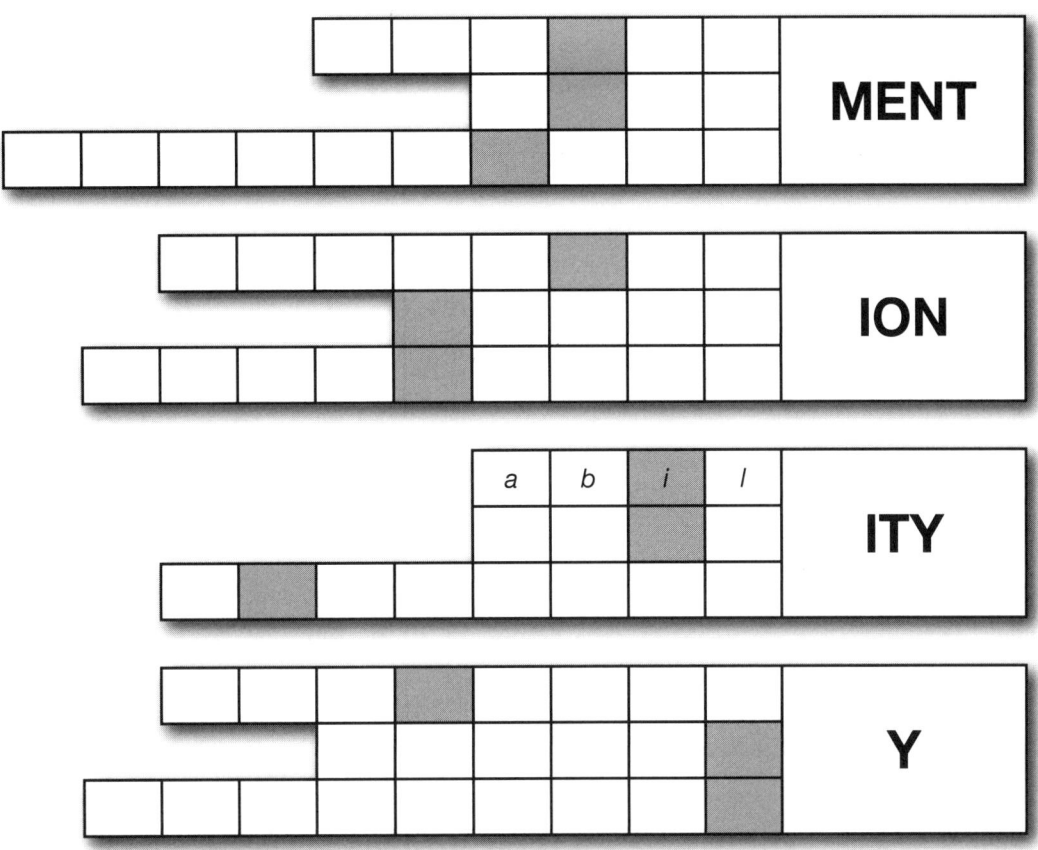

1 I was so frightened that for a moment I lost the _a_ _b_ _i_ _l_ _i_ _t_ _y_ to speak.

2 The ＿ ＿ ＿ ＿ ＿ ＿ ＿ ＿ ＿ of penicillin changed the world.

3 Her disappearance was a complete mystery. There was no ＿ ＿ ＿ ＿ ＿ ＿ ＿ ＿ ＿ ＿ ＿.

4 When Robbie came on stage, everybody started jumping with ＿ ＿ ＿ ＿ ＿ ＿ ＿ ＿ ＿.

5 Sarah didn't answer the door, but I could hear ＿ ＿ ＿ ＿ ＿ ＿ ＿ inside the house.

6 The vacation was a big ＿ ＿ ＿ ＿ ＿ ＿ ＿ ＿ ＿ ＿ ＿ ＿ ＿. The hotel was terrible, and it rained every day.

7 My great-grandfather was given a medal for ＿ ＿ ＿ ＿ ＿ ＿ ＿ during the Second World War.

8 I love watching ＿ ＿ ＿ ＿ ＿ ＿ ＿ TV shows like *The Biggest Loser*.

9 My brother is having ＿ ＿ ＿ ＿ ＿ ＿ ＿ ＿ ＿ with math at school, so he's going to work with a tutor.

10 At last I've made an important ＿ ＿ ＿ ＿ ＿ ＿ ＿ ＿! I'm going to study medicine in college.

11 She works for a volunteer ＿ ＿ ＿ ＿ ＿ ＿ ＿ ＿ ＿ ＿ that helps sick children.

12 There is a strong ＿ ＿ ＿ ＿ ＿ ＿ ＿ ＿ ＿ that it will rain tomorrow.

2 Write the highlighted letters in the boxes below. Then unscramble the letters to discover an important skill you need for playing video games. Do you have it?

| _i_ | | | | | | | | | | | |

You need good hand-to-eye ＿ ＿ ＿ ＿ ＿ ＿ ＿ ＿ ＿ ＿ ＿ ＿

Motivator quiz: How brave are you?

What would you do in the following situations? Circle the best answer for you.

1 If you saw your favorite actor or actress in the street, would you . . .

a) ask him or her out on a date?

b) ask for his or her autograph?

c) pretend you don't recognize him or her and walk away?

2 If you found a tarantula in your house, would you . . .

a) keep it as a pet and take care of it?

b) ask someone to pick it up and take it away?

c) scream and run out of the house?

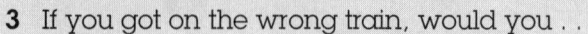

3 If you got on the wrong train, would you . . .

a) stay on it and explore somewhere new?

b) get off at the next station and catch the next train back?

c) panic, and press the emergency button?

4 If you were alone in the house and a horror movie was on the TV, would you . . .

a) turn off the lights and watch to the end?

b) watch it, but from behind a cushion?

c) turn the TV off immediately?

5 If you were in a restaurant and the waiter brought you the wrong food, would you . . .

a) give it back to the waiter and complain to the manager?

b) complain to your friends, but eat the food?

c) eat the food and not say anything?

6 If you were alone in the house at night and you heard a strange noise, would you . . .

a) go immediately and check it out?

b) call a neighbour or a friend and ask them to stay with you?

c) hide under the bed?

Add up your total and check the results:

a = 5 points   **b** = 3 points   **c** = 1 point

25–30 Bravery is your middle name! Nothing is too much for you!

12–24 You prefer not to take unnecessary risks, but are calm in a crisis.

0–11 You often panic and don't use your common sense. Relax!

Student A

1 Listen to Student B's problem. Use the cues to ask questions to get more information. Give him or her advice to solve the problem, using the suggestions in the box below.

• Which/test?   • What/time/start?   • How important/this test?   • How much/studied?

> a) Take the test anyway, and hope that the questions are easy.   b) Stay up and study all night.
> c) Study with me this evening.

2 Ask Student B for advice for the following problem. Reject his or her first suggestion, giving reasons. Decide what to do, and write your decision in the space below.

Problem: You have a virus on your computer and have lost an important school project that you have to give to your teacher tomorrow.

Decision: I'm going to _____.

> **Useful language:** *What should I do?/What would you do?*
> *If I were you, I'd . . ./Why don't you . . .?/I think you should . . .*
> *I'm not sure/I don't think that's a good idea . . .*
> *That's a good idea./Maybe you're right.*

Student B

1 Ask Student A for advice for the following problem. Reject his or her first suggestion, giving reasons. Decide what to do, and write your decision in the space below.

Problem: You have an important test tomorrow. You haven't studied for it.

Decision: I'm going to _____.

2 Listen to Student A's problem. Use the cues to ask questions to get more information. Give him or her advice to solve the problem, using the suggestions in the box below.

• When/happen?   • Which project/work on?   • How much work/have to do?   • What time/have to give it in?

> a) Buy a new computer.   b) Call a computer advice line.
> c) Apologize to your teacher and ask if you can hand in the project next week.

> **Useful language:** *What should I do?/What would you do?*
> *If I were you, I'd . . ./Why don't you . . .?/I think you should . . .*
> *I'm not sure/I don't think that's a good idea . . .*
> *That's a good idea./Maybe you're right.*

31

7A Mixed messages

Student A

1 Student B has asked you to retrieve his or her voicemail messages. Reorder the sentences below to make a message from Jo.

- [ ] bring a friend if you want! Can you
- [1] Hi, _____ . It's
- [ ] (349) 617-8652. Bye!
- [ ] need to bring anything, but can you
- [ ] Jo. I was just calling to invite
- [ ] call me back? My new number is
- [ ] my place and starts at 8:30. You don't
- [ ] you to my party on Saturday. It's at

2 Report the message from Exercise 1 to Student B. Use *she said/asked*.

"Jo called. She said she was calling to ask you to . . ."

3 Student B will give you a message. Write down the details on the notepad on the right.

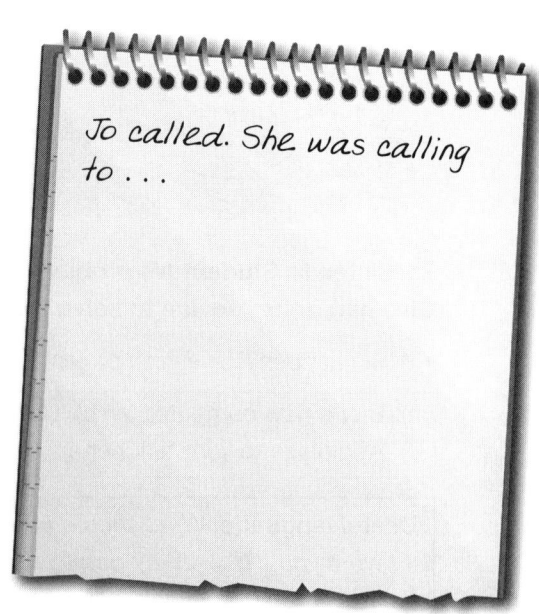

Al called. He wants to talk . . .

- -

Student B

1 Student A has asked you to retrieve his or her voicemail messages. Reorder the sentences below to make a message from Al.

- [ ] is (349)129-5521. Bye!
- [ ] your notes? Can you call me when you
- [1] Hello, _____ . This is
- [ ] difficult! Can we do it
- [ ] about our math homework. It's so
- [ ] together? Or can you lend me
- [ ] get this message? My number
- [ ] Al. I wanted to talk to you

2 Student A will give you a message. Write down the details on the notepad on the right.

Jo called. She was calling to . . .

3 Report the message from Exercise 1 to Student A. Use *he said/asked*.

"Al called. He said he wanted to talk to you about . . ."

7B School tricks

1 One of the students at Hampton High School has taken a baseball trophy from outside the school office. Read the speech bubbles, and complete the principal's notes using the verbs in the box.

a Sorry I'm late.

Lucy

b My bag's so heavy, I can't lift it!

c Yes, I'll bring it tomorrow. Sorry.

d Why don't we just ask if any of the students have seen it?

e Take that cap off right now!

f Danny, can you get the attendance sheet for me, please?

g That's not true! I wasn't there!

h I was getting some books from the library.

i Yes, it's true. I left it at home.

j I'll get the attendance sheet, sir!

admitted	~~apologized~~	asked	complained	denied	explained
offered	promised	refused	suggested	told	

Principal's notes

- Lucy ¹ _apologized_ to her teacher, Mr. Swain, for being late this morning. She arrived at 9 A.M., looking hot and tired. She ² _____ that her bag was very heavy.
- Rob arrived early at 8:30 A.M. He was wearing a New York Mets baseball cap. I ³ _____ him to take it off immediately.
- Danny arrived at 8:45 A.M. I asked him where his homework was. At first he ⁴ _____ to answer, but then he ⁵ _____ that he'd left it at home. He ⁶ _____ to bring it the next day.
- At 8:50 A.M. Mr. Swain ⁷ _____ Danny to get the attendance sheet from the school office, but Rob ⁸ _____ to go instead. He was away for more than ten minutes.
- Rob said he saw Lucy near the school office when he was getting the attendance sheet at 8:50 A.M. Lucy was angry. She ⁹ _____ being there, and ¹⁰ _____ that she was getting some books from the library.
- Miss Brown ¹¹ _____ asking the students directly if they had seen the trophy. When I asked them, nobody said anything. One of the boys, Rob, just smiled.
- Two hours later I found the trophy on top of my car, with a New York Mets baseball cap on top of it. I think there's one person who knows I'm a Yankees fan!

2 Write the names of the speakers under the speech bubbles.

3 Which student took the trophy and put it on the principal's car? _____

33

7c A-maze-ing relationships

1 Find fifteen phrases connected with relationships in the maze. The numbers indicate the first word of each phrase. You do not need to use all the words.

START ▼						
¹ make	indeed	to	⁸ have	in	engaged	to
up	with	close	a	good	⁹ get	¹⁰ get
friend	² get	⁷ be	friend	relationship	with	divorced
to	married	with	about	¹² care	a	from
³ get	an	argument	¹³ ask	with	up	¹¹ break
along	⁶ have	with	out	¹⁴ treat	child	¹⁵ go
well	a	love	in	like	a	out
with	⁴ worry	about	⁵ fall	is	need	with

▼ FINISH

1 _____make up with_____	6 _____	11 _____
2 _____	7 _____	12 _____
3 _____	8 _____	13 _____
4 _____	9 _____	14 _____
5 _____	10 _____	15 _____

2 Write the remaining eight words from the grid, then reorder them to make a famous English proverb about friendship.

_____ _____ _____ _____

_____

Read Sally's story about an argument with her friend Mike. Then complete the two telephone conversations between Sally and Mike.

I'm angry at my friend Mike. He called me on Thursday and invited me to go bowling on Saturday night, so I accepted. I asked him to call on Saturday morning to tell me where and when to meet him. He promised to call at 11.

Anyway, on Saturday morning he didn't call. I tried to call him, but his phone was off. He finally called at 7 P.M.! He apologized for not calling earlier. I asked what had happened, and he explained that he'd lost his phone. I asked him why he hadn't borrowed a phone. Then he admitted that he'd forgotten! I was really angry and told him he was just selfish. He apologized again and offered to pick me up at 7:30! Of course I refused to go, because there wasn't time to get ready. Well, he finally persuaded me to go, and I said I'd see him half an hour later. And . . . well, I'm glad I went, because I met Mike's friend Andy and now we're going out together!

Call 1

Mike: Hi, Sally! [1]_Would you like to come bowling on Saturday night_?

Sally: Oh, thanks! I'd love to! [2]_____ to tell me where and when to meet you?

Mike: Yeah, OK, [3]_____.

Sally: Great! Talk to you on Saturday, then. Bye!

Mike: Bye!

Call 2

Mike: Hi, Sally. [4]_____ sooner.

Sally: It's 7 o'clock! I've been trying to call you.
[5]_____?

Mike: [6]_____.

Sally: Why [7]_____?

Mike: Um, well to be honest, [8]_____.

Sally: What?! Mike, you're [9]_____!

Mike: I really am sorry. Anyway, [10]_____ at 7:30.

Sally: No, it's too late now. There isn't time to get ready.

Mike: Oh, please come, Sally! It'll be fun!

Sally: Oh, all right! [11]_____ in half an hour.

Mike: Great, bye!

Sally: Bye . . .

1 Complete the article with phrases from the box.

broke up	fell in love	getting along well	got engaged to	got married to	got divorced from
had a good relationship		have an argument	make up	~~was going out with~~	

Brad Pitt has been out with some of Hollywood's most beautiful women . . .

In 1993, he ¹*was going out with* film co-star Juliette Lewis, and in 1996 he ² _____ Gwyneth Paltrow, although it didn't last long.

But then, in July 2000, Brad ³ _____ *Friends* star Jennifer Aniston at a lavish wedding in Malibu, and it looked like he'd found his perfect partner. But they ⁴ _____ less than five years later, and while they were still married, the newspapers were talking about Brad's new relationship with Angelina Jolie.

It is believed that Brad ⁵ _____ with Angelina while they were working on the film *Mr. and Mrs. Smith*. They immediately ⁶ _____ with each other. At the time, Aniston and Pitt weren't ⁷ _____. Pitt finally ⁸ _____ Aniston in October 2005.

Now Brad and Angelina are constantly in the news. The newspapers tell us when they ⁹ _____ and when they ¹⁰ _____. They have six children, and Brad has adopted Angelina's children. Is Brad settling down at last?

2 Write the answers to the questions. Unscramble the highlighted letters to discover the mystery word.

1 Which TV series was Jennifer Aniston in? __ ☐ __ __ __ ☐ __

2 Where did Brad and Jennifer get married? __ __ __ ☐ __ __

3 What was the name of Brad and Angelina's first film together? *Mr. and Mrs.* __ __ __ __ ☐

4 In which month did Brad and Jennifer get divorced? __ __ ☐ __ __ __ __

3 Complete the instruction with the mystery word.

Circle every _____ word and discover the mystery fact.

On	At	In	1996	2001	2004	Angelina	Jennifer	Juliette	Jolie	Aniston
Lewis	gave	bought	started	this	one	a	big	loud	new	job
life	career	like	by	as	the	an	a	opera	pop	rock	actor
player	singer

An evening at the Odeon

1 Read the movie reviews and complete the adjectives.

---

1   After a terrible accident, 15-year-old Sami is [1]s _h_ _o_ c _k_ _e_ d to discover she is the
    only person left on the planet. She feels [2]l _ _ _ l _ and [3]f _ _ g h _ _ _ _ d, until she
    realizes that she has company after all . . . This film is so scary, I was [4]t _ _ _ _ f _ _ d
    after just ten minutes!

---

2   Mac is [5]a _ g _ _ when his wife decides to go on vacation without him. At first, he is too
    [6]p _ _ _ d to even contact his friends, but after three days he is so [7]b _ r _ _ he goes
    out – and he meets Mimi. Suddenly, everything changes . . . A [8]c h _ _ _ f _ _ movie
    with a [9]h _ _ p _ ending: I loved it!

---

3   Susan meets Rick, Rick is [10]c _ _ f _ _ _ d, so he leaves Susan, Susan is [11]s _ _ _,
    and Rick is [12]d _ _ r _ _ s _ d. It's the usual story. I was [13]t h _ _ _ l _ d to receive
    free tickets for this movie, but I left before the end. And I was [14]a _ n _ _ e d because I
    missed the last bus home. Very disappointing.

---

4   All the animals are [15]e _ c _ t _ d because the King of the Jungle is coming back, and his
    mother is [16]w _ _ _ i _ d that the monkeys will ruin the party. This movie is funny and full
    of surprises. I was [17]a _ u s _ _ because the adults enjoyed the movie as much as the
    children, and I'm not [18]a s _ _ m _ d to say I loved it, too!

---

2 Match the reviews to the posters.

8B New life

1 Read Jack's e-mail, and complete the sentences with the correct form of *used to*, *get used to*, and *be used to*.

From: jackflash@awol.com

To: rebs@yesmail.com

Subject: New life!

Hi Rebecca! How are you? Sorry I missed your call. I ¹*'m not used to* getting calls during the day, so my phone was turned off. Everything is going very well here in Italy, and I'm getting along great with my host family. Life is very different in the U.S., so I'm trying to ² _____ doing things differently.

The food is great! At home in Portland, I never ³ _____ have breakfast, but here I have a big breakfast. I never ⁴ _____ drink tea at home, so I ⁵ _____ having coffee . . . no change there. And it didn't take me long to ⁶ _____ eating pasta every day, because I love it!

I ⁷ _____ this hot weather, though! I've always liked the rain and cold back home in Portland. Here in August, it's sometimes over 30°C. I don't know if I'll ever ⁸ _____ that.

Do you remember Mark Jones? We ⁹ _____ be in the same class at school. I saw him at the city center yesterday. He's studying at the same university, too. He looked very tired. I think he ¹⁰ _____ studying so many hours every day!

Keep in touch!—Jack

---

2 Answer the questions about Jack.

1 Where is he from? ☐☐☐☐☐☐☐☐

2 Which country is he in now? ☐☐☐☐☐

3 What does he drink at breakfast? ☐☐☐☐☐☐

4 Where does he study? ☐☐☐☐☐☐☐☐☐☐

3 Write the highlighted letters from Exercise 2 in the boxes below. Then unscramble the letters to find out where Jack is.

☐☐☐☐☐☐ _____

Copyright © 2011 by Pearson Education, Inc. Permission granted to photocopy for classroom use.

Jimmy's bad week

1 Complete Jimmy's blog with phrasal verbs from the box.
Then write the correct day on each picture.

broken in	fit in	give in	hand in	~~moved in~~	stay in

1 Monday April 27th 4:10 P.M.
We've ___moved in___ to the new house.
There are boxes everywhere. Chaos.

2 Tuesday April 28th 6:25 P.M.
First day at my new school. Disastrous. All
the other students know each other. And they
all have MP3 players. I don't _____.

3 Wednesday April 29th 5:50 P.M.
Another bad day at school. I forgot to
_____ my math homework. ANGRY
teacher.☹

4 Thursday April 30th 7:20 P.M.
Can it get any worse? Dad heard about my
math homework. He won't let me go out. I
have to _____ tonight and tomorrow.

5 Friday May 1st 9:05 P.M.
Bored. I told Mom and Dad what I
want for my birthday on Sunday,
but they say it's too expensive and
they won't _____. ☹☹

6 Saturday May 2nd 1:15 P.M.
Mom and Dad are taking me to a
restaurant to celebrate my birthday.
I wanted to go to a movie!

Saturday May 2nd 10:10 P.M.
NO NO NO NO! Burglars
_____ to the house! They
took my birthday present (and the
TV, the stereo, the computer . . .)

Monday

Please!   NO!

2 Look at the final picture and blog entry. What
happened on Sunday, May 3? _____

Sunday May 3 09:10 A.M.
The best birthday ever! The burglars didn't steal my
present . . . Mom and Dad are great!

Student A

1 Read the article about the Titanic and complete the numbered spaces with *so* or *such*.

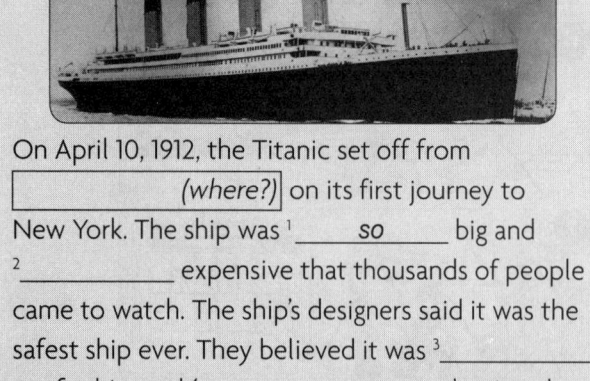

On [_____(when?)_], the Titanic set off from Southampton on its first journey to [_____(where?)_]. The ship was ¹____so____ big and ²_____ expensive that thousands of people came to watch. The ship's designers said it was the safest ship ever. They believed it was ³_____ a safe ship, and ⁴_____ strong, that it only had 20 lifeboats.

But four days later, on [_____(when?)_], the Titanic hit a huge iceberg. The ship was

⁵_____ heavy that it was impossible to turn it away from the iceberg, which was ⁶_____ big, that it made an enormous hole. There was ⁷_____ much damage that the Titanic started sinking.

Some people didn't realize what had happened because they were having ⁸_____ an enjoyable evening. But soon they understood. The Titanic took no more than three hours to sink. In fact, it sank ⁹_____ quickly that when another ship, the Carpathia, arrived to help, it found just [_____(how many?)_] survivors in lifeboats. A total of 1,523 people died in the disaster.

2 Ask Student B questions to complete the information in the boxes. Then answer Student B's questions.

- -

Student B

1 Read the article about the Titanic and complete the numbered spaces with *so* or *such*.

On April 10, 1912, the Titanic set off from [_____(where?)_] on its first journey to New York. The ship was ¹____so____ big and ²_____ expensive that thousands of people came to watch. The ship's designers said it was the safest ship ever. They believed it was ³_____ a safe ship, and ⁴_____ strong, that it only had [_____(how many?)_] lifeboats.

But four days later, on April 14, the Titanic hit a huge iceberg. The ship was ⁵_____ heavy

that it was impossible to turn it away from the iceberg, which was ⁶_____ big, that it made an enormous hole. There was ⁷_____ much damage that the Titanic started sinking.

Some people didn't realize what happened because they were having ⁸_____ an enjoyable evening. But soon they understood. The Titanic took no more than [_____(how long?)_] to sink. In fact, it sank ⁹_____ quickly that when another ship, the Carpathia, arrived to help, it found just 705 survivors in lifeboats. A total of [_____(how many?)_] people died in the disaster.

2 Answer Student A's questions, then ask Student A questions to complete the information in the boxes.

1 Complete the conversations with phrases from the box.

so happy	so lazy	so lucky	so much	so much time	so nice
so quickly	so selfish	so tired	~~so upset~~	such a beautiful	such a great

1 I'm ¹ *so upset*. I don't know what to do!

What's the problem?

2 It's Jimmy. He's ² _____. He even forgot my birthday last week!

3 Oh, dear. My Jack's ³ _____. He gave me ⁴ _____ ring on my birthday.

4 And I'm ⁵ _____ because there's ⁶ _____ cleaning to do. Jim's ⁷ _____, he never does anything.

5 Really? Jack's wonderful. We do the cleaning ⁸ _____ because he's ⁹ _____ helper.

6 Jimmy spends ¹⁰ _____ with his friends, I rarely see him.

7 Jack's always ¹¹ _____ to stay at home that he never sees his friends! I'm ¹² _____!

2 Look at the final frame and complete Jack's sentence using *such + adjective*.

8 I'm having _____ time that I'll be back at midnight! Don't wait up!

9A What did she have done?

1 Sarah went into town this morning. Match the cards and receipts to the sentences below. Then complete the sentences using causative *have*.

A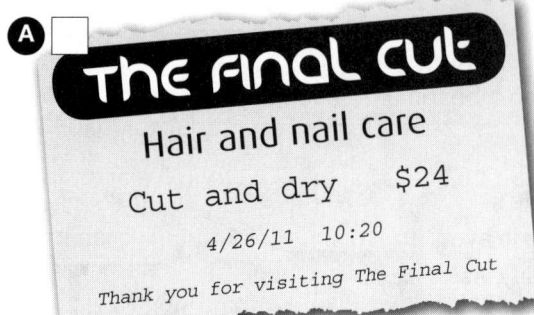

THE FINAL CUT
Hair and nail care
Cut and dry $24
        4/26/11   10:20
Thank you for visiting The Final Cut

B

PAYNE&MERCY
Dental Practice
Your next appointment is on
Monday 4/26 at 10:30 a.m.
(check up, clean, and polish)

C 1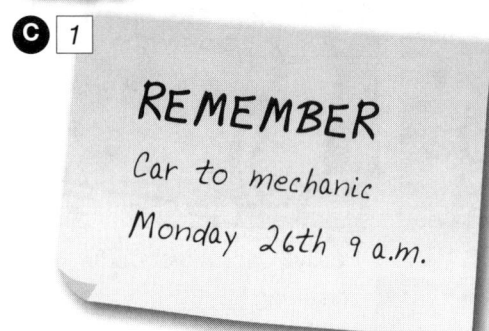

REMEMBER
Car to mechanic
Monday 26th 9 a.m.

D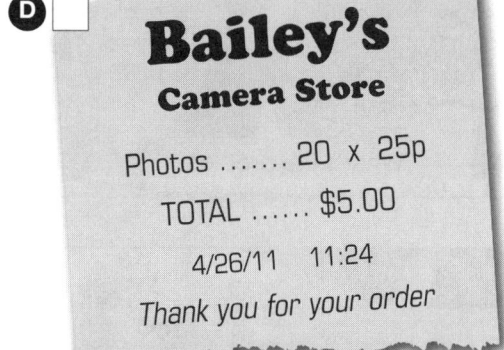

Bailey's
Camera Store
Photos .... 20 x 25p
TOTAL $5.00
    4/26/11   11:24
Thank you for your order

E

wash'n'go
car wash service
Full wash $20
    4/26/11   12:30

F

The Copy Shop
Photocopies......$0.45
    4/26/11   9:35

1 At 9 A.M. Sarah went to the mechanic to __*have her car repaired*__ (car/repair).

2 She walked to the copy shop and _____ (documents/photocopy).

3 At 10 A.M. her sister called her while she _____ (hair/cut).

4 At 10:25 she went to the dentist to _____ (teeth/clean and polish).

5 Then she _____ (photos/print) at Bailey's.

6 By 12:35 she _____ (car/wash).

2 Where did she go after having her photos printed and before having her car washed?

_____

3 Trace Sarah's route through town from her house.

9B Suffixes crossword

1 Complete the crossword puzzle with the adjective form of the nouns in the clues.

Across

2 mystery (10)
3 suspicion (10)
7 beauty (9)
8 use (6)
9 attraction (10)
11 ambition (9)
13 sun (5)
14 origin (8)
15 humor (8)

Down

1 danger (9)
2 music (7)
4 imagination (11)
5 salt (5)
6 effect (9)
10 thirst (7)
12 wonder (9)

2 Find words from the crossword clues and answers to complete the favorite movies.

This week, movie director John Howard tells us his all-time favorites.

My Top Five Movies

Manhattan Murder [1]M_____, starring Woody Allen and Diane Keaton (1993)

It's a [2]W_____ *Life*, starring James Stewart (1946)

[3]D_____ *Liaisons*, starring Michelle Pfeiffer and John Malkovich (1988)

American [4]B_____, starring Kevin Spacey (1999)

Empire of the [5]_____, starring Christian Bale and John Malkovich (1987)

9c The birthday present

1 Look at the pictures and circle the two adjectives that match the objects.
Put a cross (X) next to the word that doesn't belong.

a) (soft) (fluffy) slippery X

e) smooth   star-shaped   oblong

b) straight   smooth   prickly

f) straight   rough   hard

c) round   thin   silky

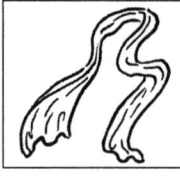

g) rectangular   round   smooth

d) rectangular   rough   hard

h) thin   fluffy   slippery

2 Write the words that don't belong in the boxes below. Then write the letters into the number code.

a)

1 S	5 L	6 I	7 P	7 P	8 E	2 R	9 Y

e)

3	14	5	3	15	13

b)

1	10	3	3	4	11

f)

1	4	2	16	6	13	11	4

c)

2	3	12	13	11

g)

2	8	17	4	16	15	13	12	5	16	2

d)

2	3	12	15	18

h)

19	5	12	19	19	9

1	2	3	4	5	6	7	8	9	10	11	12	13	14	15	16	17	18	19

3 Use the code to find out what Ellis got for his birthday.

19 – 3 – 3 – 4 – 14 – 16 – 5 – 5 _____

1 Read the tourist forum about York in the U.K. Complete the entries with the phrases in the boxes.

1
feel as if   feel like you've   ~~isn't like~~   look and sound
it seems as if   smells terrible

The ▓▓▓▓▓▓▓ in York [1] _isn't like_ any other museum. You [2]_____ you're going back in time when you travel backwards in a "time capsule". Suddenly [3]_____ you've arrived in a busy village . . . and you have! But in 975 AD. The air [4]_____ as you go past the dirty farmhouses and animals, and the models of people [5]_____ real. When you come out, you really [6]_____ lived a part of Viking life. Great! *Rating:* ✶ ✶ ✶ ✶ ✶
John, London, U.K.

2
feels warm   felt as if   looks beautiful   looked like   seem very busy
seemed so   smells delicious   tasted awful

Whatever you do in York, don't visit ▓▓▓▓▓▓▓. It [7]_____ from the outside, and in fact when you go in it [8]_____ and inviting, and the food [9]_____. But don't be fooled. Our food [10]_____ it had come straight from the freezer, and it [11]_____. The place didn't [12]_____, but the service was terrible. We [13]_____ we weren't wanted because the staff [14]_____ unfriendly. Never again! *Rating:* ✶
Julia, Atlanta, U.S.

3
feel like   feel like you can't
look and taste   seem expensive
seems very busy   sounds interesting

My favorite part of York is the tiny but ancient shopping street called ▓▓▓▓▓▓. Even the name [15]_____! At first, it [16]_____ and chaotic. But that's the point. It's so small, and there are so many people, that you might [17]_____ go into the stores! But don't miss one of the lovely tea stores. They might [18]_____, but they're worth every penny. The tea and cakes [19]_____ wonderful, and the service will make you [20]_____ a VIP! Fantastic!

Rating: ✶ ✶ ✶ ✶

Alice, Los Angeles, U.S.

---

2 Match the photographs with the descriptions. Write the places in the forum above.

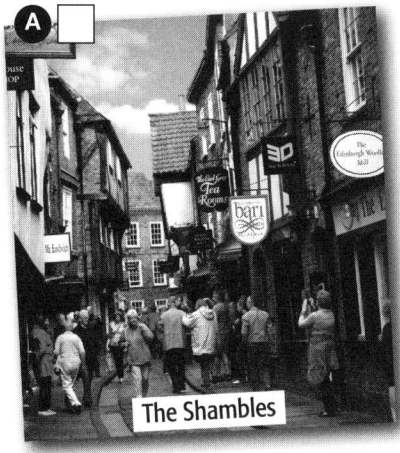
A   The Shambles

B   The Jorvik Center

C   Weyland Restaurant

9D Consolidation 2 Something wrong

Student A

1 You have the following problems. Go to the store or restaurant. Explain the problem to Student B, who works there, and make a request.

. . . fix the flat tire?

. . . give me a discount?

> **Useful language**
>
> *I have a (few) problem(s) with . . .*
> *There's something wrong with . . .*
> *Could you . . .?/Would you mind __ing?/*
> *Do you think you could . . . ?*

2 Ask about Student B's problems, and respond to his or her requests. You can agree to one request, but offer alternative solutions for the other one.

> **Useful language**
>
> *What is wrong with it/them?   What seems to be the problem?   Sure, that won't be a problem.*
> *I'll see what I can do.   I'm not sure I can do that. What about . . . ?*

Alternative solutions: • repair it   • choose a different bike   • exchange it for the same model

--- ✂ --

Student B

1 Ask about Student A's problems, and respond to his or her requests. You can agree to one request, but offer alternative solutions for the other two.

> **Useful language**
>
> *What is wrong with it/them?   What seems to be the problem?   Sure, that won't be a problem.*
> *I'll see what I can do.   I'm not sure I can do that. What about . . . ?*

Alternative solutions: • lend you a pump   • choose a different dish   • have a free dessert

2 You have the following problems. Go to the store. Explain the problem to Student A, who works there, and make a request.

. . . lower the seat?

. . . exchange it for a better model?

> **Useful language**
>
> *I have a (few) problem(s) with . . .*
> *There's something wrong with . . .*
> *Could you . . .?/Would you mind __ing?/*
> *Do you think you could . . .?*

10A An important appointment

1 Look at the pictures. Then complete the sentences with the correct form
of the verbs from the box using *should have* or *ought to have*.

| a ☐ | b ☐ | c ☐ | d ☐ |

| e ☐ | f 1 | g ☐ | h ☐ |

| bring | make | not eat | put | not leave | not go | take | ~~wear~~ |

1 I _should have worn_ more comfortable shoes.

2 I _____ a taxi.

3 I _____ shrimp last night.

4 I _____ the alarm for earlier.

5 I _____ to bed so late last night.

6 I _____ the map at home.

7 I _____ an umbrella.

8 I _____ an appointment with the hairdresser.

2 Match each sentence to the correct picture.

3 Fill in the gap to complete the story.

Maybe you should have _____ in the afternoon!

Modern mysteries

1 Read the news articles. The phrasal verbs are mixed up! Write the phrasal verbs in the correct places in the articles.

ALIENS LEAVE TRASH IN CENTRAL PARK

An alien spaceship landed in Central Park yesterday evening. Joggers and dogwalkers were surprised when a bright light appeared in the sky. The sky was so bright they [1] ~~threw away~~ _looked away_. A local police officer said, "I walked up to the door of the spaceship, but when it started to open, I [2] **put away** _____ as fast as I could. I was terrified!" Witnesses say that a small green man came out, walked around, then went back inside and closed the door. The spaceship [3] **passed away** _____ a few minutes later. This morning, scientists were analyzing the contents of a small plastic bag they found at the scene. "It seems that the aliens [4] **got away** _____ their trash while they were here," they laughed.

DEAD MILLIONAIRE RETURNS

Jack Ruddle, a millionaire from Texas, [5] **looked away** _____ 20 years ago when he was 80 years old. Before he died, he [6] **ran away** _____ all his money to the local museum. Now it seems he wants it back! Last night John Smith, the museum warden, found an old man in the museum. "He had a flashlight in his hand, and he was clearly looking for something," he said. "When he saw me, he [7] **went away** _____ his flashlight and left. He was very quick for his age. I tried to catch him, but he [8] **gave away** _____." When Mr. Smith returned, he found a note that said "I want my money back!" – and it was signed by Jack Ruddle!

2 Write the answers to the questions in the spaces below.

1 Where did the spaceship land? __ __ __ __ __ __ __   __ ☐ __ __

2 What color was the alien? __ __ ☐ __ __

3 What was in the plastic bag? __ __ __ ☐ ☐

4 How many years ago did Jack Ruddle die? __ __ __ __ __ __

5 Where was Jack Ruddle from? __ __ ☐ __ __ __

6 What did the old man leave at the museum? __ ☐ __ __ __

3 Unscramble the letters in the boxes to give an explanation for the mysteries!

The stories must be __ __ __ __ __ __ !

10c The suspect

1 Circle the word that doesn't belong in each group of words.

1	burgle	steal	rob	(suspect)
2	mug	write graffiti	charge	steal
3	accused	convicted	vandalized	suspected
4	pickpocket	vandal	thief	shoplifter
5	police officer	burglar	accomplice	bank robber
6	prison	thief	mugger	shoplifter
7	burgle	rob	mug	deny
8	committed	arrested	admitted	denied

2 Write the words that don't belong from Exercise 1 in the box. Then use the words to complete the police interview below.

> suspect,

Officer: So where were you last night at 10:30 P.M.?

Joe: I was at home with my girlfriend.

Officer: Do you ¹ _____ that you were near the train station?

Joe: The train station?

Officer: Yes. Last night a ² _____ broke the windows of some offices opposite the station.

Joe: Well, it wasn't me!

Officer: But somebody saw you in that area at that time.

Joe: It can't have been me. I was at the movies!

Officer: At the movies? So you weren't at home, with your girlfriend?

Joe: Um. That was later.

Officer: You had an accomplice. A short man, with curly hair. A ³ _____ in the area saw you together.

Joe: I don't know a short man with curly hair.

Officer: We ⁴ _____ this man early this morning. He's in the cell next door. He says he was with you.

Joe: He must be lying. It wasn't me.

Officer: He says you ⁵ _____ the offices near the train station, and then you took the bus home.

Joe: That's not true!

Officer: You could go to ⁶ _____, you know.

Joe: Why do you ⁷ _____suspect_____ me? You don't have any evidence.

Officer: Look at these photos. Do you recognize that man?

Joe: Well, yes. That's me!

Officer: Yes, Joe. And they're from the security cameras opposite the train station! I am going to ⁸ _____ you with vandalizing property on Station Road.

Excuses, excuses, excuses!

Student A

1 Read the situations, and complain to Student B. Respond to his or her excuses.

1 You have tickets for an important football game. Student B offered to give you a ride. The game starts at 3 P.M. and it takes 20 minutes to get to the stadium. At last he or she arrives at 2:55 P.M.
2 You arrive home from school and find the kitchen in a mess, with food burning in the oven. Student B is watching TV in the living room.
3 You lent Student B your favorite white T-shirt, but when he or she gives it back, it is pink!

2 Listen to Student B's three complaints, and respond with the excuses in the pictures.

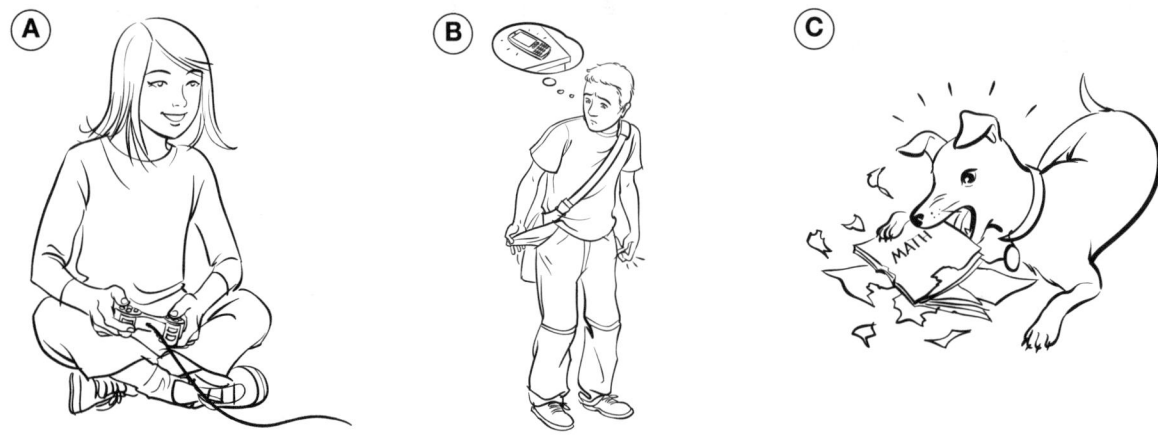

A   B   C

✂ -

Student B

1 Listen to Student A's three complaints, and respond with the excuses in the pictures.

A   B   C

2 Read the situations, and complain to Student A. Respond to his or her excuses.

1 You have the starring role in the school play. Student A promised to come and watch the play but arrived just before the end.
2 Student A promised to call you this morning to arrange to meet, but he or she didn't call. You tried to call, but he or she didn't reply. He or she finally calls at 3 P.M.
3 You lent your math book to Student A. When he or she gives it back it is dirty, wet, and torn.

Crime					
Sentence					

Read the clues and figure out which criminal committed what crime and what his punishment was.

- Three of the criminals went to prison, and two paid fines.
- The pickpocket has been in prison for 11 months and is looking forward to going home next month.
- Pete admitted that he hadn't paid for a box of chocolates he got at the supermarket.
- One criminal went to prison for five years.
- Max didn't go to prison. He has never stolen anything in his life.
- When the police arrested Alec, he was running down the street with a man's wallet. The man hadn't even noticed!
- One of the criminals was arrested at night behind the train station. He was throwing stones and breaking windows.
- The shoplifter paid a fine of $2,000.
- Jake usually committed his crimes at night. Police found stolen televisions, stereos, and computers in his garage.
- The bank robber got the longest prison sentence.
- The vandal paid a fine of $800 to cover the damage.
- Ron committed his crime 12 years ago. He'll be released in three years.

1 Unscramble the anagrams to complete the article.

Are we obsessed with the news?

¹ _Newspapers_ (PARSENPEWS) in Britain have always been read by thousands of people. Over 3 million copies of *The Sun*, Britain's most popular ² _____ (BOLTAID), are sold daily, and the famous newspaper *The Times*, which was founded in 1785, is read by approximately 600,000 people.

But newspaper sales are falling, and people's obsession has been satisfied in new ways. Some TV news ³ _____ (LENNACHS) give people updates every 15 minutes. And the Internet is used by more and more people to read the news, 24 hours a day. ⁴ _____ (SHINEDALE) are transmitted to cell phones and computer desktops, and ⁵ _____ (ROSTIDE) have been quick to put their newspapers and even ⁶ _____ (AMINGAZES) online. Many ⁷ _____ (STOPCADS) are downloaded every day so that listeners can choose when they want to hear the news.

The news is becoming interactive. ⁸ _____ (STROPER) and photos are sent daily to news sites by members of the general public. Thousands of ⁹ _____ (GLOBS) have been created over the last few years, in which people are reporting, commenting on, and discussing the news.

2 Write the words from Exercise 1 in the spaces below.

1 n e w s |p| a p e r s

2 _ |²| _ _ _ _ _

3 _ _ |³| _ _ _ _ _

4 _ _ _ _ _ _ _ _

5 _ _ |⁴| _ _ _ _

6 _ _ _ |⁵| _ _ _ _

7 _ _ _ |⁶| _ _ _ _

8 |⁷| _ |⁸| _ _ _ _

9 _ _ _ _ _

3 Write the highlighted letters in the boxes below. (Use the numbers to help you.) Then unscramble the letters to find the least popular people in the media. One letter is used twice.

|¹ p| |²| |³| |⁴| |⁵| |⁶| |⁶| |⁷| |⁸| _____

11B Have your say!

1 Read the opinions posted on an Internet discussion site.

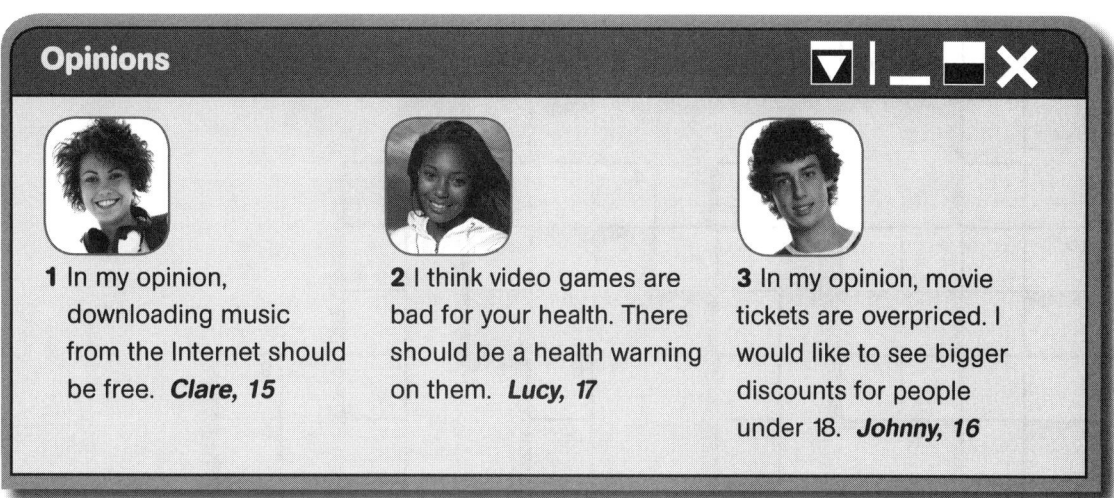

Opinions

1 In my opinion, downloading music from the Internet should be free. *Clare, 15*

2 I think video games are bad for your health. There should be a health warning on them. *Lucy, 17*

3 In my opinion, movie tickets are overpriced. I would like to see bigger discounts for people under 18. *Johnny, 16*

2 Complete the responses with words or phrases from the box.

agree	OK, but	see what	sorry, but	~~that's a great~~	think so
too	way	you're right			

Responses

A	B	C
¹ I think *that's a great* idea. CDs are much too expensive. **1**	⁴ Maybe _____, but is there medical evidence for this?	⁷ Sorry, I don't _____. Movies are very expensive to make.
² Me _____! Last time I went, I paid $10, and the movie was awful!	⁵ _____ how will the record companies make money?	⁸ _____ I think you're wrong. If we don't pay, bands will stop making records.
³ I _____, too. I have friends who are obsessed. They spend hours in virtual worlds.	⁶ I _____ you mean, but most theaters already give discounts to young people.	⁹ No _____! In fact, many people say they are good for coordination and reflexes.

3 Match each A, B, or C response to an opinion from Exercise 1.

4 Are you a rebel, a diplomat, or a yes-person? Choose the answers in columns A, B, or C that reflect your personal opinion. Then read the results below.

Mostly As: You're a yes-person. You often agree with people, but only if what they say is in your interest, too!
Mostly Bs: You're a diplomat. You are very good at seeing both sides of the story.
Mostly Cs: You're a rebel. You like to be different. You often disagree with people just to be different.

Noun and adjective crossword

1 Complete the crossword puzzle with the noun or adjective form of the clues.

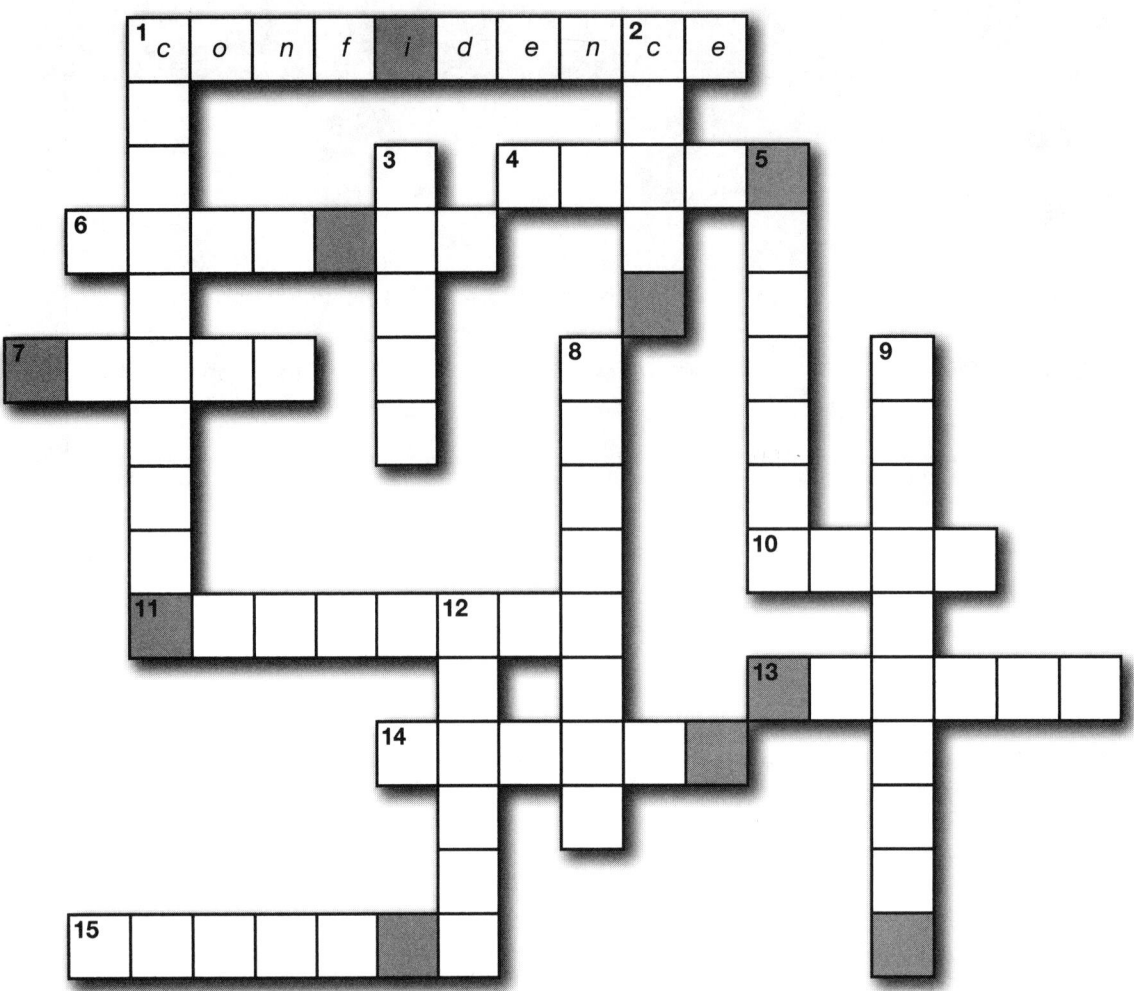

	1 c	o	n	f	i	d	e	n	2 c	e

Across – nouns
1 confident
4 young
6 brave
7 angry
10 lucky
11 strong
13 wise
14 beautiful
15 poor

Down – adjectives
1 courage
2 cruelty
3 pride
5 hope
8 truth
9 success
12 greed

2 Find the letters in the highlighted squares above to complete the famous proverb.

Early to bed, Early to rise, Makes a person _h_ _e_ _a_ _ _ _ _ _ _y_,
_w_ _e_ _ _ _ _t_ _h_ _ _, *and* _ _ _ _ _ !

Student A

Use the cues to ask Student B questions to complete the article.
Take turns asking the questions in number order.

This week in *The Best of British* we discover the history of Britain's favorite car – the Mini!

The first Mini was produced on [1] *August 26, 1959* (*when?*). It was designed by Sir Alec Issigonis. A small, cheap car was needed because [3] _____ (*why?*) at that time. When the Mini Cooper was launched in 1961, the [5] _____ (*what?*) started being used.

In the 1960s, the Mini was adopted as a fashion accessory by famous celebrities, such as [7] _____ (*which?*). In 1969 it was featured in the successful movie *The Italian Job.*

By the year 2000, [9] _____ (*how many?*) cars had been manufactured and sold all over the world. The final "original" model of the Mini was produced in October 2000. But in [11] _____ (*when?*) a new version of the Mini was launched, and Britain's favorite car is being enjoyed again by people all over the world.

✂ -

Student B

Use the cues to ask Student A questions to complete the article.
Take turns asking the questions in number order.

This week in *The Best of British* we discover the history of Britain's favorite car – the Mini!

The first Mini was produced on August 26, 1959. It was designed by [2] *Sir Alec Issigonis* (*who?*). A small, cheap car was needed because gas was being rationed at that time. When the [4] _____ (*what?*) was launched in 1961, the name "Mini" started being used.

In [6] _____ (*when?*) the Mini was adopted as a fashion accessory by famous celebrities, such as The Beatles. In 1969 it was featured in the successful movie [8] _____ (*which?*).

By the year 2000, 5.3 million cars had been manufactured and sold all over the world. The final "original" model of the Mini was produced in [10] _____ (*when?*). But in 2001 a new version of the Mini was launched, and [12] _____ (*what?*) is being enjoyed again by people all over the world.

Motivator quiz: the United States of America

Circle the correct answers. Check your answers and write your score.

1 How many people visit Disneyland in California every year?

a) less than 8 million   **b)** between 8 million and 14 million

c) more than 14 million

2 Which musical city in the U.S. was destroyed by a hurricane in 2005?

a) Miami   **b)** Chicago   **c)** New Orleans

3 Which building was destroyed in September 2001?

a) the Empire State Building   **b)** the World Trade Center   **c)** Sears Tower

4 How many times have the Summer Olympic Games been held in the U.S.?

a) twice   **b)** three times   **c)** four times

5 What food is usually eaten at a traditional Thanksgiving dinner in the U.S.?

a) chicken   **b)** beef   **c)** turkey

6 Which famous park can be seen from the top of the Empire State Building?

a) Central Park   **b)** Madison Square Gardens   **c)** Yosemite National Park

7 Which city do earthquake experts say will be hit one day by "The Big One"?

a) Boston   **b)** Washington, D.C.   **c)** San Francisco

8 Which U.S. president was assassinated in 1963?

a) George Bush   **b)** John F. Kennedy   **c)** Bill Clinton

9 Which of these American actors has been nominated for the most Oscars?

a) Jack Nicholson   **b)** Robert De Niro   **c)** Dustin Hoffman

10 Which Austrian-born actor was elected Governor of California in 2003?

a) Clint Eastwood   **b)** Ronald Reagan   **c)** Arnold Schwarzenegger

My score: _____

9–12	You aren't just an expert on the U.S. – you possibly *are* American!
5–8	You know the U.S. pretty well. Have you been there on vacation?
1–4	The U.S. is not your favorite subject!

12A Money, money, money!

1 Complete the paragraphs with the correct form of the verbs from the box.

borrow	donate	earn	go (x 2)	inherit	
invest (x 2)	lend	lose	make	owe	pay
repay (x 2)	save	spend (x 2)	splurge	win	

Mike, Dave, and Jim are brothers.

Mike had $20,000. He ¹ _____spent_____ half of it on a new car, and he ² _____ $5,000 of it and got a 20 percent return on his investment. When their mother died, all three brothers ³ _____ $2,000. Mike ⁴ _____ half of this to charity. With the rest of his inheritance he ⁵ _____ on a beautiful diamond ring for his wife. She was very happy!

Dave works for a bank and ⁶ _____ a good salary. He puts money in the bank every month, and so far he ⁷ _____ $12,000. Last week, he decided to sell his old car to a friend and ⁸ _____ $1,500. A few months ago, his brother Jim asked him for help to ⁹ _____ a debt, so Dave ¹⁰ _____ him $4,000. He ¹¹ _____ the inheritance from his mother on a moped for his daughter. A few years ago, Jim had $10,000 in savings, which he ¹² _____ in a local business. Unfortunately, it recently ¹³ _____ bankrupt, so he ¹⁴ _____ all his savings. He also ¹⁵ _____ the bank $5,000. If he ¹⁶ _____ some money from his brother Dave and used half of his inheritance to ¹⁷ _____ the bank debt, he probably ¹⁸ _____ bankrupt himself! Then suddenly, his luck changed! He ¹⁹ _____ $50,000 in the lottery! So he ²⁰ _____ his brother back, but he hasn't decided what to do with the rest of the money yet!

2 How much money do the three brothers have now?

Mike $ _____   Dave $ _____   Jim $ _____

12B Pete and Olivia's world trip

1 Complete Pete's thoughts with verbs from the box.

learn	order	~~use~~	stay	take	wear

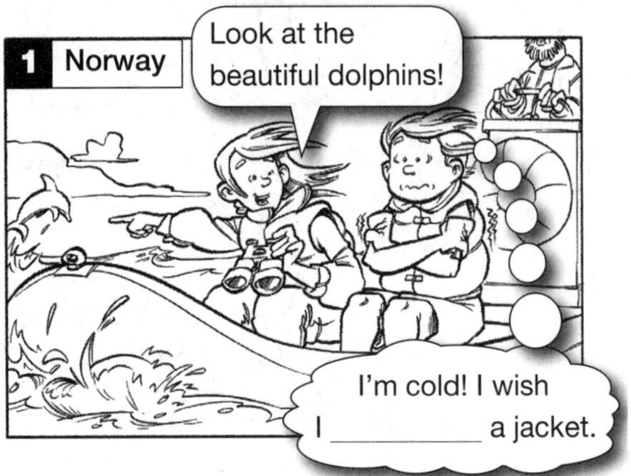

1 Norway

Look at the beautiful dolphins!

I'm cold! I wish I _____ a jacket.

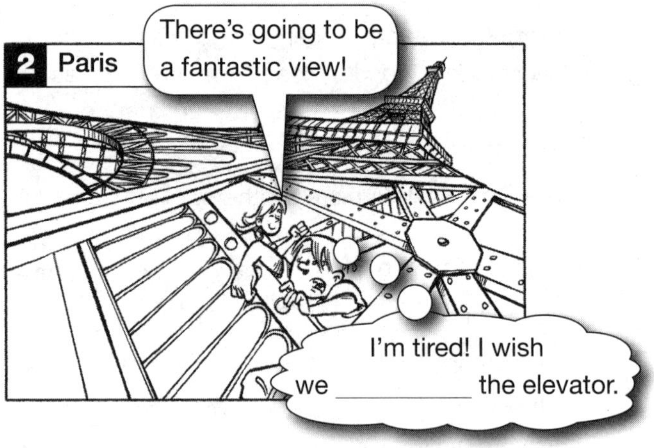

2 Paris

There's going to be a fantastic view!

I'm tired! I wish we _____ the elevator.

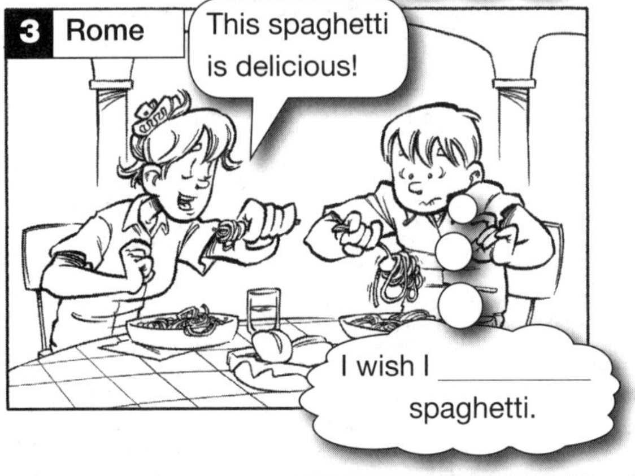

3 Rome

This spaghetti is delicious!

I wish I _____ spaghetti.

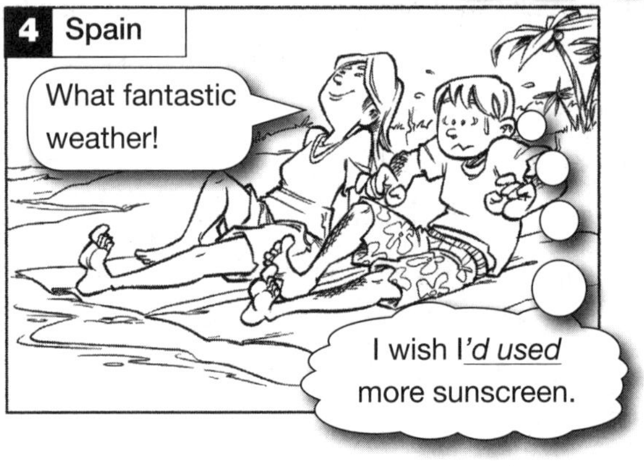

4 Spain

What fantastic weather!

I wish I'*d used* more sunscreen.

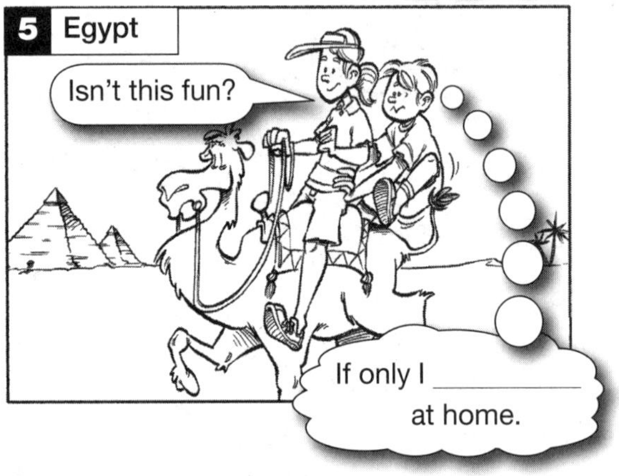

5 Egypt

Isn't this fun?

If only I _____ at home.

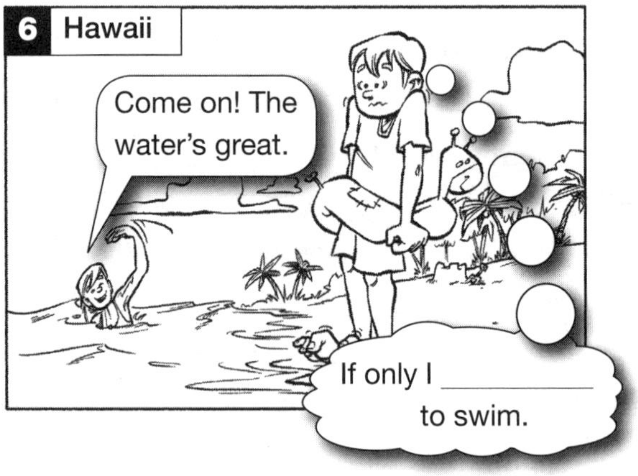

6 Hawaii

Come on! The water's great.

If only I _____ to swim.

2 Look at the final picture and complete Olivia's thought.

7 London

It's great to be home!

I wish I _____ in Hawaii.

12c *Congratulations!*

1 Complete the conversations with words from the box.

~~believe~~	can't	day	deserve	fantastic	great
guess	have	must	never	thrilled	true

1. **Sam:** Hi, Ben. How was the audition for the Harry Potter film?

   Ben: ¹ _Believe_ it or not, I got the part!

   Sam: ² _____ job! That's ³ _____!

   Ben: Thanks. I ⁴ _____ believed it would happen.

2. **Holly:** Hi, Jo. You look happy!

   Jo: I ⁵ _____ believe it! I've won a trip to Australia.

   Holly: Congratulations! You must be ⁶ _____.

   Jo: Thanks. It ⁷ _____ have been my lucky ⁸ _____!

3. **Matt:** ⁹ _____ what. I've been accepted to Harvard University!

   Teacher: Wow! Congratulations! You ¹⁰ _____ it.

   Matt: Thanks. I couldn't ¹¹ _____ done it without you.

   Teacher: That's not ¹² _____! You worked really hard.

2 Match the conversations to the pictures.

3 Put the pieces in order, and write the letter below. Who is it to?

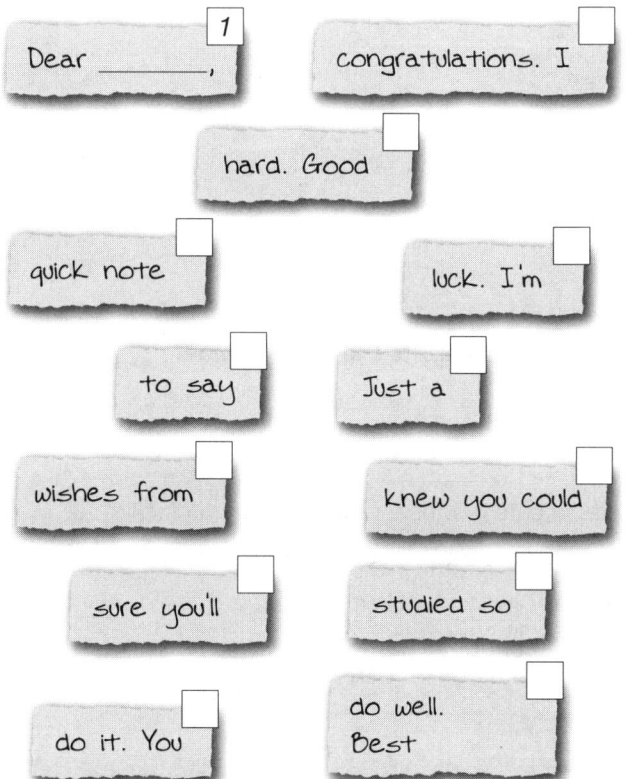

Dear _____ , ⟨1⟩

congratulations. I

hard. Good

quick note

luck. I'm

to say

Just a

wishes from

knew you could

sure you'll

studied so

do it. You

do well. Best

Dear _____

_____

_____

_____

_____

_____

_____

_____

Mr. Jackson

1 Complete the talk show interview using an *if* clause and the past perfect.

Host: Well, on today's show we have singer Kate Crawford. Kate, you say that you became famous because of a single decision that changed your life?

Kate: Yes! I used to have a job in a bank in Manhattan, but I worked very long hours. A friend invited me to a party one night. I was very tired, but I decided to go anyway. If I ¹ *hadn't gone* (not go) to that party, I ² *would still have been* (still be) at the bank.

Host: So what happened?

Kate: Well, it was a great party and I didn't get home until 2 A.M. I ³ _____ (not stay) so late if ⁴ _____ (not be) such a good party. I went straight to bed and forgot to set my alarm clock. I had to get up at 6:30 A.M., but I didn't wake up until 9! If I ⁵ _____ (not get) home so late, I'm sure I ⁶ _____ (not forget) to set my alarm clock.

Host: So you were late for work?

Kate: Yes. And if I ⁷ _____ (not be) late for work, I ⁸ _____ (not lose) my job.

Host: You lost your job? So what did you do next?

Kate: I took a part-time job in a karaoke club. It wasn't ideal, but if I ⁹ _____ (not take) it, I ¹⁰ _____ (not be able) to pay the bills. One evening I was bored, so I got up and sang a song by Frank Sinatra. I ¹¹ _____ (not do) that if there had been more people in the club. I didn't realize there was a record producer in the club at the time!

Host: And if he ¹² _____ (not hear) you sing, he ¹³ _____ (not offer) you the record contract. So you have to thank your friend for having that party!

Kate: Yes, and my boss for firing me!!

2 Write the answers to the questions. Unscramble the highlighted letters to discover the mystery word.

1 Where was the bank? __ __ __ [ ] __ __ __ __ __ __

2 What kind of club did she work in? __ __ [ ] __ __ __ __ __

3 Who was the song by? __ __ __ __ __   __ [ ] __ __ [ ] __ __

4 Who was in the club? __ __ __ __ __ __   __ __ __ [ ] __ __ __ __

3 Complete the instruction with the mystery word. Then write the words below to discover a mystery fact!

Circle every _____ word.

shoes   Chicago   (top)   record   Kate   model   café   Moss   Naomi   nightclub
sing   Campbell   have   America   was   party   Claudia   discovered   actress
Madonna   while   as   that   she   them   work   was   walked   missed
shopping   friend   people   in   never   dance   London

_____ *Top* _____

Complete the crossword puzzle with the missing words from the sentences.

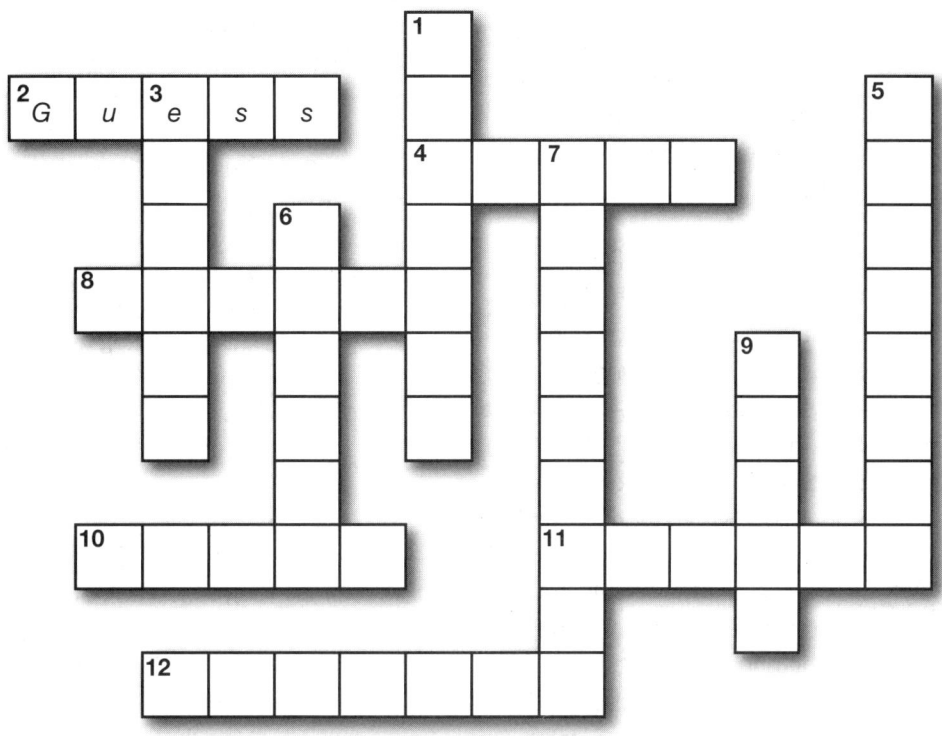

Conversation 1

Janine: Hey! _____Guess_____ what! I just won
$50,000 in the lottery. (2 across, 5)

Carly: Congratulations! That's incredible!

Janine: It must have been my _____
day. (4 across, 5)

Carly: What are you going to do with the money?

Janine: Well, I'll probably _____ some of
it to charity. (8 across, 6)

Carly: That's a good idea.

Janine: And then I'm going to _____ out
these old clothes and buy some new ones.
(9 down, 5)

Carly: Great! A shopping trip!

Janine: That's right. And then I think I'll
_____ on a new car. (12 across, 7)

Carly: Fantastic! Let's _____! (7 down, 9)

Conversation 2

Josh: Hey! You look happy!

Mick: Yeah! _____ (1 down, 7) it or not,
I have great news! I just _____ out
that I got a new job. (10 across, 5)

Josh: Fantastic! You must be thrilled.

Mick: Yeah, I never believed it would _____.
(6 down, 6) Now I can pay back the money
I _____ from my brother last year.
(5 down, 8)

Josh: Great!

Mick: Yes! We're going to _____ tonight
at that new Mexican restaurant. Do you
want to come? (3 down, 3, 3)

Josh: I'd love to. But it's expensive . . . can you
_____ it? (11 across, 6)

Mick: Yes! I have a job now!

Teacher's notes and Answer keys

1A Shop until you drop

Aims: To practice vocabulary for clothes and accessories

Instructions: Ex 1 • Give each S a photocopy of the worksheet. • Draw Ss' attention to the example answer g) (*sweatshirt*). • Ss unscramble the letters to find the rest of the clothes and accessories and write them in the list.

Ex 2 • Explain that the Ss have to figure out who bought which items. • Read the first and second clues: *One of the girls bought a new sweatshirt for when she goes jogging* and *Kirsty and Owen never play sports*, and elicit from the students who bought the sweatshirt (*Martha*). Point out the example answer. • Ss work in pairs, read the clues and figure out who bought which items.

Ex 3 • Ask Ss to check that the items in the column under Kirsty's name are correct. • Draw Ss' attention to the price tags in the pictures, and ask how much she spent on the headband ($2.50). • Ss find the prices of all the items and write how much each person spent.

> **Answer key: Ex 1** 1 sweatshirt g) 2 fleece a)
> 3 suit f) 4 bracelets h) 5 bandana c) 6 leggings k)
> 7 cargo pants d) 8 tie i) 9 tights l) 10 flip flops b)
> 11 headband j) 12 high heels e)
> **Ex 2** 1 Kirsty: headband, high heels, tights, bandana
> 2 Mick: cargo pants, fleece 3 Martha: sweatshirt,
> flip flops, bracelets, leggings 4 Owen: suit, tie
> **Ex 3** 1 Kirsty: $44.99 2 Mick: $58.00 3 Martha:
> $51.40 4 Owen: $97

1B Figure it out!

Aims: To practice vocabulary for jobs and professions

Instructions: Ex 1 • Give each S a photocopy of the worksheet. • Draw Ss' attention to the pictures and the example answer in the grid (*chef*). • Ask them to identify the picture that represents the word *chef* (the chef's hat). • Point out the letter grid below and show them that *c* corresponds to the number *1*. • Look at the first picture with the Ss and

elicit which job it represents (*police officer*). The Ss find the correct place in the frame to write the word, and write it in. • Ss work in pairs to identify all the jobs from the pictures and write them in the correct place in the frame, using the picture clues to help them. They then write the letters in the grid, matching each letter to the correct number.

Ex 2 • Ss use the letters from the code to create the proverb.

> **Answer key: Ex 1** carpenter, detective, doctor, chef, hairdresser, teacher, police officer, journalist, musician, ski instructor
> Code: 1 C 2 S 3 I 4 F 5 T 6 J 7 E 8 O 9 R 10 M
> 11 U 12 H 13 L 14 N 15 A 16 K 17 P 18 V 19 D
> **Ex 2** Many hands make light work.

1C The right job

Aims: To practice adjectives to describe work

Instructions: Ex 1 • Give each S a photocopy of the worksheet. • Draw Ss' attention to the example answer in the first job advertisement (*glamorous*). • Ss unscramble the letters to find the rest of the adjectives to complete the job advertisements.

Ex 2 • Draw Ss' attention to the online interview conversation. • Ask the Ss to read the conversation in pairs. • Ss re-read the advertisements and write down the job Jake has applied for.

> **Answer key: Ex 1** 1 glamorous 2 boring
> 3 dangerous 4 stressful 5 tiring 6 interesting
> 7 well-paid 8 educational 9 worthwhile 10 rewarding
> 11 dull 12 badly paid 13 creative 14 exciting
> **Ex 2** reporter

1D Consolidation 1 Can I help you?

Aims: To review the language for shopping for clothes

Instructions: • Make a photocopy of the worksheet for each pair of Ss. • Cut the worksheets in half along the dotted line. • Arrange the Ss in pairs, Student A and Student B. • Give each student the Student A or Student B section of the worksheet.

Ex 1 • Draw Student As' attention to the first picture, and Student Bs' attention to the situation and the clothes and prices he or she has in the "store". • Ask a Student A to ask for the object in the picture as he or she would in a store (*I'm looking for some cargo pants*). • Encourage Student Bs to look at the list of clothes, and ask a Student B to respond (*What size?*). • Cue Ss to build the conversation, and encourage them to write down the price of the items they "buy". • Ss role-play the situations for all the items.

Ex 2 • Ss change roles and repeat the procedure for Ex 1.

Ex 3 • Ask Ss to add up how much money they spent and compare with each other.

1D Consolidation 2 The train journey

Aims: To review the use of tag questions

Instructions: Ex 1 • Give each S a photocopy of the worksheet. • Draw Ss' attention to the picture story. Ask them to read the speech bubble in the first frame, and indicate the example tag question. • Read the second frame and elicit the correct tag question (*are we?*). Ask the Ss to write the tag in the bubble. • Ss read the story and write in the remaining tags, then compare with a partner.

Ex 2 • Invite Ss to suggest how the boy is feeling throughout the conversation (*bored, annoyed, irritated, angry*). • Draw the Ss' attention to the speech bubbles, and explain they are the boy's responses to each question. • Indicate the first response. • Ss work in pairs to match the responses to the frames.

> **Answer key: Ex 1** 1 isn't it? 2 are we? 3 aren't you? 4 doesn't she? 5 don't they? 6 isn't it? 7 doesn't he? 8 have you?
> **Ex 2** 1 e 2 g 3 c 4 a 5 d 6 f 7 h 8 b

2A What happened?

Aims: to practice the language for showing concern and reassuring

Instructions: Ex 1 • Give each S a photocopy of the worksheet. • Draw Ss' attention to the first line of Conversation 1. • Ask them to locate 8 across on the crossword, establish the number of letters (4). • Ask Ss to suggest the answer, and point out the example answer on the crossword. • Ss read the two conversations and complete the crossword.

Ex 2 • Ss write the highlighted letters from the crossword in the boxes, then unscramble them to complete the proverb.

> **Answer key: Ex 1** Across: 2 hand, 6 all right, 7 love, 8 hurt, 10 problem, 12 fine, 14 better; Down: 1 yourself, 3 anything, 4 happened, 5 worry, 9 really, 11 balance, 13 sure
> **Ex 2** Actions speak louder than words.

2B Growing up

Aims: to practice phrasal verbs with *up*

Instructions: • Give each S a photocopy of the worksheet. • Look at the pictures and establish the situation. Ask Ss "What is the relationship between the woman and the boys?" (mother and sons), and "What time is it?" (early morning). • Ss look at the pictures and match them to conversations a)–h). • Draw Ss' attention to conversation a) and the example answer. • Ss complete the rest of the conversation with the correct phrasal verbs from the box, changing the form as necessary.

> **Answer key:** 1 b Wake up 2 d Get up 3 c Pick up 4 h Stand up 5 g look up 6 f hurry up 7 a take up 8 e grow up

2C Lucy's vacation blog

Aims: To practice the simple past and past perfect

Instructions: Ex 1 • Give each S a photocopy of the worksheet. • Draw Ss' attention to Lucy's blog and the example answer for 1 (*got*). • Ss complete the blog using the verbs in the box in the simple past or past perfect forms.

Ex 2 • Look at the list of forms of transportation and ask Ss to identify the forms of transportation Lucy used on her trip. • Read the first paragraph again, and ask the Ss "How did they travel?"

(by car), "Where from?" (home), and "Where to?" (Sea-Tac Airport). • Ss number the forms of transportation in the correct order, according to the blog.

> **Answer key: Ex 1** 2 started 3 had forgotten 4 had missed 5 called 6 was 7 found 8 asked 9 got 10 had arrived 11 took 12 had checked 13 had left
> **Ex 2** 1 car 2 taxi 3 train 4 tram 5 airplane

2D Consolidation 1 Born to sail

Aims: To practice the narrative tenses

Instructions: • Make a photocopy of the worksheet for each pair of Ss. • Cut the worksheets in half along the dotted line. • Arrange the Ss in pairs, Student A and Student B. • Give each student the Student A or Student B section of the worksheet. • Show the Ss that there is information about Ellen MacArthur on the worksheets. • Ask the first example question for Student A, using the cue *how old?* (*How old was she in 1980?*) and ask a Student B to answer it (*four years old*). Show Ss A the example answer. • Ask the first example question for Student B, using the cue *who?* (*Who did she go with?*) and ask a Student A to answer it (*her aunt*). Show Ss B the example answer on the worksheet. • The Ss take turns asking and answering the questions in pairs and writing the information. • Ss compare their completed worksheets to check their answers.

2D Consolidation 2 Motivator quiz: transportation

Aims: To review the vocabulary for transportation

Instructions: • Give each S a photocopy of the quiz. • Ss answer the quiz questions individually. • Check answers with the whole class. • The Ss count up their total and read their result.

> **Answer key:** 1 c) yellow 2 c) a type of boat 3 c) a type of bicycle (that two people can ride, with two seats and two sets of handlebars and pedals) 4 b) between 1,000 and 2,000 (about 0.91 every minute) 5 a) in the 18th century 6 a) flying airplanes 7 c) Aston Martin 8 b) the world's fastest train (top speed 361mph) 9 c) Paris to Istanbul 10 b) the official airplane of the U.S. president

3A Potato pancakes

Aims: To practice vocabulary for food and kitchen equipment

Instructions: Ex 1 • Give each S a photocopy of the worksheet. • Draw Ss' attention to the circled example (*spoon*), and ask Ss what the other three words have in common (they are all pieces of equipment used for preparing food, not for eating it). • Ss work in pairs to identify and circle the words that don't belong. • Check answers with the whole class, and encourage Ss to justify their choices.

Ex 2 • Ss use the words that don't belong from Ex 1 to complete the recipe.

Ex 3 • Draw Ss' attention to the picture of the shopping basket and the shopping list. • Ask students to identify the sour cream in the basket. • Ss match the remaining items in the basket to the items on the list, and identify the ingredient that Jo has forgotten.

> **Answer key: Ex 1** 1 spoon 2 bowl 3 salt 4 eggs 5 frying pan
> **Ex 2** 1 bowl 2 eggs 3 salt 4 frying pan 5 spoon
> **Ex 3** a) cheese b) sour cream c) 1 red pepper d) shrimp e) 2 lemons f) mushrooms
> Jo has forgotten the salmon.

3B Odd jobs

Aims: To practice vocabulary for part-time jobs

Instructions: Ex 1 • Give each S a photocopy of the worksheet. • Draw Ss' attention to the circled job in the grid and the example answer below (*dog walking*). • Point out that the second job must start in a box next to the last word of the first job, and ask Ss to find it (*teaching*). • They then complete and circle the job (*teaching computer skills*) and add it to the list. Tell Ss that not all the words in the grid are used. • Ss find and circle the rest of the jobs, and complete the list.

Ex 2 • Ss find the remaining eight words in the grid. • They use the words to complete the job advertisement.

> **Answer key: Ex 1** 1 dog walking 2 teaching computer skills 3 mowing lawns 4 weeding yards 5 delivering newspapers 6 working in a store 7 washing cars 8 helping in a retirement home 9 babysitting
> **Ex 2** 1 on 2 meeting 3 people 4 friendly 5 money 6 having 7 jobs 8 helping 9 yard 10 pets

3C I'm sorry, but . . .

Aims: To practice inviting, accepting, and refusing with excuses

Instructions: • Make a photocopy of the worksheet for each pair of Ss. • Cut the worksheets in half along the dotted line. • Arrange the Ss in pairs, Student A and Student B. • Give each student the Student A or Student B section of the worksheet.

Ex 1 • Draw Student As' attention to the text message in the picture cues, and Student Bs' attention to the box with reasons why they may be busy. • Ask a Student A to read the situation in the message and express it as an invitation. • Ask a Student B to apologize, choose a reason for not going, and express it as an excuse. • If necessary, use the board to build the sample conversation. • Ss role-play the three situations.

Ex 2 • Ss change roles and repeat the procedure for Ex 1.

3D Consolidation 1 Teen troubles

Aims: To review *make*, *let,* and *allowed (to)*, and review *should* and *ought to*

Instructions: Ex 1 • Give each student a photocopy of the worksheet. • Draw Ss' attention to the first problem, and read it up to the end of the example answer. • Read the next sentence and elicit the answer using the correct structure of *make*, *let*, or *allowed ('s allowed to)*. Remind Ss that the answers can be positive or negative. • Ss complete the three problems.

Ex 2 • Draw Ss' attention to reply a). • Elicit which problem it responds to (Problem 3). Ask Ss to try to give a reason for their answer. • Ss work in pairs to match the remaining replies to the problems.

Answer key: Ex 1 1 won't let me 2 's allowed to 3 'm not allowed to 4 makes me 5 lets me 6 won't let her 7 make her 8 isn't allowed to 9 let me
Ex 2 a) problem 3 b) problem 1 c) problem 2 d) problem 2 e) problem 3 f) problem 1

3D Consolidation 2 Who does what?

Aims: To review vocabulary for part-time jobs

Instructions: • Give each student a photocopy of the worksheet.• Draw the Ss' attention to the pictures, and explain that they have to figure out which friend does which job. • Read the first clue, *Neither Ben nor Dan need any special skills for their jobs*, and elicit from the Ss which jobs in the chart need special skills (*teaching computer skills* and *painting and decorating*). Point out the Xs that eliminate Ben and Dan from these jobs. • Ss work in pairs, read the clues, and figure out who does which job through a process of elimination.

Answer key: a) Cassie – painting and decorating b) Ellie – dog walking c) Ben – delivering daily newspapers d) Alec – teaching computer skills e) Marta – mowing lawns f) Dan – helping in a retirement home

4A The best vacation ever

Aims: To practice superlatives with present perfect

Instructions: Ex 1 • Give each S a photocopy of the worksheet. • Draw Ss' attention to the first picture frame and elicit the situation (*boy telling friend about vacation*). • Ask Ss to read sentence a) with the example answers. Point out the use of the superlative form of the adjective in parentheses and the present perfect form of the verb in parentheses. • Ss complete the remaining sentences with superlatives and present perfect. • Ss check answers in pairs, then as a class. • Ask Ss to look at the first picture frame again, and ask them which sentence it corresponds to (sentence a). Point out the example answer. • Ss work in pairs to match the rest of the sentences to the pictures.

Ex 2 • Ss use their imagination to complete the story in their own way.

Answer key: Ex 1 a) best, 've ever had b) most comfortable, 've ever been c) most expensive d) whitest, sandiest e) most exciting f) most dangerous, 've ever seen
Frame 1 a) Frame 2 e) Frame 3 d) Frame 4 b) Frame 5 f) Frame 6 c)
Ex 2 Possible answers: the most exciting/boring vacation, 's ever had / the most beautiful place, 's ever been

65

4B Music matches

Aims: To practice vocabulary for musical instruments and musical terminology

Instructions: Ex 1 • Give each S a photocopy of the worksheet. • Draw Ss' attention to the example answer (*album*), and point out that there is an extra letter (*d*). • Ss unscramble the letters to find the rest of the music vocabulary and complete the magazine excerpts.

Ex 2 • Point out the letter *d* from the example in Ex 1 in the box. • Ss write the remaining letters in the box. • They then rearrange the letters to find the name of a musical instrument.

> **Answer key: Ex 1** 1 album 2 band 3 songwriters 4 backup singers 5 rapper 6 lead singer 7 lyrics 8 songs 9 single 10 charts 11 beat 12 producer
> **Ex 2** double bass

4C The dinner party

Aims: To practice restrictive and nonrestrictive relative clauses

Instructions: Ex 1 • Give each S a photocopy of the worksheet. • Draw the Ss' attention to the picture of the people at the dinner party, and explain that Ss have to figure out the people's jobs and where they are from. • Read the first clue, *Ross, who is sitting between a man on his right and a woman on his left, has acted in 20 movies,* and the example answer in the chart (*movie star*). • Ss work in pairs, read the rest of the clues, and figure out the jobs and the cities to complete the chart.

Ex 2 • Read the first clue to the Ss again. • Draw their attention to the table plan, and ask which man is Ross (*at the left end of the table*). • In pairs, Ss work out the seating plan from the clues. Then they write the names on the plan.

Ex 3 • Ss use the clues and the seating plan to discover the murderer, victim, and witness.

> **Answer key: Ex 1** Ross is a movie star from London, Marina is an artist from Moscow, Kate is a doctor from New York, Andreas is an opera singer from Rio de Janeiro, Leo is a musician from Lima, Carla is a movie star from Rome.

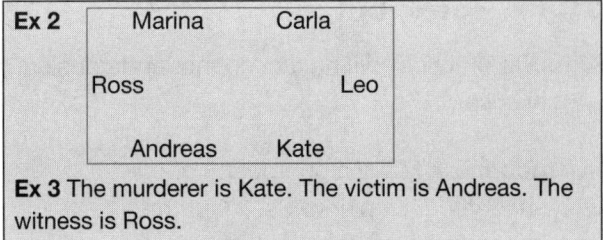

> **Ex 2**
> Marina   Carla
> Ross   Leo
> Andreas   Kate
>
> **Ex 3** The murderer is Kate. The victim is Andreas. The witness is Ross.

4D Consolidation 1 Good news, bad news

Aims: To review reacting to good and bad news, and superlatives with present perfect

Instructions: Ex 1 • Give each S a photocopy of the worksheet. • Read Will's first line and point out the example answer (*long*). • Draw the Ss' attention to the letter c) in the box, and explain that this refers to Jade's answer. Ask Ss to find Jade's answer c) and read it. • Then return to Will's second line. Ss continue the process until they have the complete conversation.

Ex 2 • Draw Ss' attention to the example answer and indicate its corresponding number on the left. • Ss write their answers in the grid to discover where Jade went on vacation.

> **Answer key: Ex 1** 1 c, long   2 f, awful   3 b, happened 4 d, bad   5 h, horrible   6 a   7 e, cheer   8 i, That's 9 g, Good
>
> **Ex 2**
>
> Jade went on vacation to Edinburgh.

4D Consolidation 2 Stars from North America

Aims: To practice present perfect and present perfect continuous

Instructions: • Make a photocopy of the worksheet for each pair of students. • Cut the worksheets in half along the dotted line. • Arrange the Ss in pairs,

Student A and Student B. • Give each student the Student A or Student B section of the worksheet.

Ex 1 • Explain that Ss have information about either Avril Lavigne or Justin Bieber on their worksheets. • Draw Ss' attention to the cue questions in the information box. • Ss read the information and complete the column for their singer.

Ex 2&3 • Make the first example question for Students A (*When was Justin Bieber born?*), and ask a Student B to answer it (*in March 1994*) • Show the Ss A where to write the information. • Repeat the procedure for Students B. • The Ss take turns asking and answering questions in pairs and writing the information on their worksheets.

Ex 4 • Ss compare the information about the two singers and write three things they have in common.

> **Answer key: Ex 4** They are both from Ontario, Canada; they are both singers; they both act.

5A Dream vacations in the U.S.

Aims: To practice vocabulary for landforms and the environment

Instructions: Ex 1 • Give each S a photocopy of the worksheet. • Draw Ss' attention to the example answer (*coast*). • Point out that the number of dashes corresponds to the number of letters needed to complete each word. • Ss write the remaining words to complete the three vacation advertisements.

Ex 2 • Read the first description of Jessica and Susie. • Elicit suggestions from the Ss for their ideal vacation (*Vacation C*). Encourage the Ss to give reasons. (*Because they love being active, because they would like to spend some time in the countryside.*) • Ss read the other descriptions, and match the people to the vacations.

> **Answer key: Ex 1** 1 coast 2 River 3 harbor
> 4 coastline 5 cliffs 6 ocean 7 desert 8 mountains
> 9 waterfalls 10 Valley 11 lakes 12 forest
> **Ex 2** Jessica and Susie: vacation C, Bill and Zoe: vacation A, Reynaldo and Lucia: vacation B

5B Disaster crossword!

Aims: To practice vocabulary for extreme weather and natural disasters

Instructions: Ex 1 • Give each S a photocopy of the worksheet. • Draw Ss' attention to the clue for 1 down, and ask them to locate 1 down on the crossword. • Point out the number of letters (9), and elicit the answer to the clue (*avalanche*). • Ss write the correct answer in the crossword. • Point out that some clues are pictures. • Ss complete the rest of the crossword.

Ex 2 • Draw the Ss' attention to the highlighted squares in the crossword. • The Ss rearrange the letters from the highlighted squares to find the name of the volcano.

> **Answer key: Ex 1 Across:** 3 hurricane 6 storm 7 hail
> 9 downpour 12 volcanic eruption 14 landslide
> 15 thunder
> **Down:** 1 avalanche 2 famine 3 heat wave 4 drought
> 5 earthquake 8 tornado 10 tsunami 11 blizzard
> 13 flood
> **Ex 2** Vesuvius

5C Camping trip

Aims: To practice vocabulary for camping equipment

Instructions: • Make a photocopy of the worksheet for each pair of Ss. • Cut the worksheets in half along the dotted line. Arrange the Ss in pairs, Student A and Student B. • Give each student the Student A or Student B section of the worksheet. • Show Ss that they each have a picture of a camping scene, but with some objects in different positions. • Ask a Student A "Is there a compass in your picture?" (Yes, there is). Then ask "Where is it?" (On the table). • Ask a Student B the same question and then "Is your compass on the table?" (No, it isn't. It's under the table, next to the camping stove). • Draw Ss' attention to the number next to the compass and the example answer. • Indicate that they should write the position of the objects in their picture when they are different from their partner's. • The Ss take turns to ask and answer and find eight differences between their pictures, writing the numbers on the worksheet and recording the differences in their notebooks.

5D Consolidation 1 Best friends?

Aims: To review making and responding to requests

Instructions: Ex 1 • Give each S a photocopy of the
worksheet. • Draw Ss' attention to the example answer
in Conversation 1. • Ss read the mini conversations
and match the requests to the conversations. • Ss
then write the requests in the spaces.

Ex 2 • Ask Ss to look at the pictures and establish
the situation. Ask Ss to identify Emily and Nick
in the pictures. • Ask two students to read the
first mini-conversation, then elicit which picture it
corresponds to (picture D). • Ss work in pairs and
match the pictures to the conversations.

Ex 3 • Ask Ss to read the conversations in pairs.
• Draw Ss' attention to the final picture, and
ask them how Nick feels (annoyed). • Ss use
their imaginations to complete the final mini-
conversation in their own words.

5D Consolidation 2 Motivator quiz: geography and the natural world

Aims: To review vocabulary for landforms and
the environment, extreme weather and natural
disasters, and to review superlatives

Instructions: • Give each S a photocopy of
the worksheet. • Ss answer the quiz questions
individually. • Check answers with the whole class.
• The Ss count up their total and read their score.

6A Phrasal verbs puzzle

Aims: To practice transitive phrasal verbs

Instructions: • Give each S a photocopy of the
worksheet. • Draw Ss' attention to the first sentence
and example answer. • Indicate the circled answer in
the puzzle (turn on). • Point out that the prepositions
may be above, below, or next to the verb. • Ss read
the remaining sentences, find and circle the phrasal
verbs in the puzzle, and complete the sentences.

6B If I were you . . .

Aims: To practice giving and responding to advice

Instructions: Ex 1 • Give each S a photocopy of
the worksheet. • Draw attention to example box 1.
• Ask Ss to identify which piece of the letter follows
and write 2 in the box. • Ss then number the rest of
the pieces in the correct order. • Show Ss where to
write the correctly ordered letter.

Ex 2 • Ss read the complete letter. • Ask Ss to
find the answer to the first question (Friday). Show
Ss where to write the answer. • Point out the
highlighted letters and numbers (e.g. 1 F). • Then
indicate the boxes in Ex 3 and the letter F in the
first box. • Ss answer the remaining questions.

Ex 3 Ss write the highlighted letters in the correct
boxes and discover the reason for Isa's problems
with Tracy.

6C Suffix scramble

Aims: To practice noun suffixes

Instructions: Ex 1 • Give each S a photocopy of the worksheet. • Draw Ss' attention to the first sentence and example answer (*ability*). • Point out that the number of dashes indicates the number of letters in the noun. Show Ss where to write answers for *-ment*, *-ion*, *-ity*, and *-y* nouns in the boxes. (The order of the boxes corresponds to the order of the sentences.) • Ss read and complete the sentences and write the correct nouns in the boxes.

Ex 2 Draw Ss' attention to the highlighted letters in the boxes in Ex 1. • Ss write the highlighted letters in the boxes in Ex 2. • The Ss rearrange the letters to find another noun to complete the sentence.

Answer key: Ex 1 1 ability 2 discovery 3 explanation
4 excitement 5 movement 6 disappointment
7 bravery 8 reality 9 difficulty 10 decision
11 organization 12 possibility
Ex 2 coordination

6D Consolidation 1 Motivator quiz: How brave are you?

Aims: To review *if* clause + past and transitive phrasal verbs

Instructions: • Give each S a photocopy of the quiz. • Ss work individually to answer the questions. • Ss add up their total and read the results. • Ss compare their answers with a partner.

6D Consolidation 2 What should I do?

Aims: To practice asking for, giving, and responding to advice

Instructions: • Make a photocopy of the worksheet for each pair of Ss. • Cut the worksheets in half along the dotted line. • Arrange the Ss in pairs, Student A and Student B. • Give each student the Student A or Student B section of the worksheet.

Ex 1 • Draw Student Bs' attention to their problem, and Student As' attention to the cue questions. • Ask a Student B to explain the problem. • Ask a Student A to form the first question. • Ask another Student B to invent an answer. • Draw Student As' attention to the suggestions a)–c), and ask a Student A to suggest a solution. • Ask a Student B to reject the solution using the correct language. Build the conversation on the board if necessary. • Ss work in pairs, Student A asking questions and suggesting solutions until Student B accepts. • Indicate where Student Bs should write their chosen solutions.

Ex 2 • Repeat the procedure for Student A's problem.

7A Mixed messages

Aims: To practice the language for leaving and taking a phone message, and reported speech

Instructions: • Make a photocopy of the worksheet for each pair of Ss. • Cut the worksheets in half along the dotted line. • Arrange the Ss in pairs, Student A and Student B. • Give each student the Student A or Student B section of the worksheet.

Ex 1 • Explain to the Ss that they have different messages on their sections of the worksheet, and that the messages are mixed up. • Draw Ss' attention to the first part of each message (with example answer 1). • Ss reorder the different parts to create their message.

Ex 2 • Ask Ss A "Who is your message from?" (*Jo*). • Draw their attention to the beginning of the message ("Jo called. She said . . ."). Ask a Student A to complete the message (*her party*). • Show Ss B where to write the message. • Ss A continue to use reported speech to give Ss B the message.

Ex 3 • Repeat the procedure for Ex 2 with Ss B.

Answer key: Student A, Ex 1 6, 1, 8, 5, 2, 7, 4, 3
Student B, Ex 1 8, 6, 1, 4, 3, 5, 7, 2

7B School tricks

Aims: To practice reported speech and verbs of reporting

Instructions: Ex 1 • Give each S a photocopy of the worksheet. • Read the situation, and draw Ss' attention to Lucy's speech bubble (*Sorry I'm late.*). • Ask them to look at the verbs in the box and decide which one corresponds to Lucy's words (*apologized*). Then indicate the example answer in the principal's notes. • Ss work in pairs to complete the rest of the headmaster's notes.

Ex 2 • Draw Ss' attention to the example answer (*Lucy*) for speech bubble a) in Ex 1. • Ss then read the complete notes and write the names under the rest of the speech bubbles.

Ex 3 • Ss work in pairs to read the notes and work out who took the trophy.

> **Answer key: Ex 1** 1 apologized 2 complained 3 told
> 4 refused 5 admitted 6 promised 7 asked 8 offered
> 9 denied 10 explained 11 suggested
> **Ex 2** a Lucy b Lucy c Danny d Miss Brown e the
> principal f Mr. Swain g Lucy h Lucy i Danny j Rob
> **Ex 3** Rob

7C A-maze-ing relationships

Aims: To practice words and phrases for relationships

Instructions: Ex 1 • Give each S a photocopy of the worksheet. • Draw Ss' attention to the circled phrase and the example answer below (*make up with*). • Point out that the words in each phrase are always adjacent to each other in the grid and that the first word of each phrase is numbered. Tell Ss that not all words in the grid are needed. • Ss find and circle the rest of the phrases, and complete the list.

Ex 2 • Ss find the remaining eight words in the grid. • They rearrange the words to create the proverb.

> **Answer key: Ex 1** 1 make up with 2 get married to
> 3 get along well with 4 worry about 5 fall in love with
> 6 have an argument with 7 be close to 8 have a good
> relationship with 9 get engaged to 10 get divorced
> from 11 break up with 12 care about 13 ask out
> 14 treat like a child 15 go out with
> **Ex 2** A friend in need is a friend indeed.

7D Consolidation 1 An argument

Aim: To review reported statements and questions

Instructions: • Give each S a photocopy of the worksheet. • Ss read Sally's story in the speech bubble. • Ask Ss some simple comprehension questions: "Who did Sally argue with?" (her friend Mike), "When did Mike call her?" (Thursday), "When did they go out?" (Saturday), "Why was Sally angry?" (Because Mike forgot to call her). • Draw Ss' attention to the first line of Call 1 and the example first part of answer 1. Ask Ss to identify the rest of the equivalent part of the conversation in the speech bubble. • Ask Ss to complete what Mike says and write it in the space. • Ss then use the rest of Sally's story to complete the two calls.

> **Answer key:** 1 Would you like to come bowling on
> Saturday night? 2 Could/Can you call me on Saturday
> morning . . . ? 3 I'll call [you] at 11. 4 Sorry I didn't
> call [you] . . . 5 What happened? 6 I lost my phone.
> 7 . . . didn't you borrow one/a phone? 8 . . . I forgot
> 9 . . . just selfish! 10 I'll/I can pick you up . . . 11 I'll
> see you . . .

7D Consolidation 2 Hollywood heartthrob

Aim: To review vocabulary for describing relationships

Instructions: Ex 1 • Give each S a photocopy of the worksheet. • Draw Ss' attention to the example answer 1 (*was going out with*) in the article. • The Ss complete the rest of the text with the phrases from the box.

Ex 2 • Ss use the completed text from Ex 1 to answer the comprehension questions and find the mystery word in the highlighted letters.

Ex 3 • Ss write the mystery word from Ex 2 into the instruction. • Check that Ss have the correct answer (*third*) before they continue. • Demonstrate to Ss by counting and circling the word *In*. Elicit the next word (*2004*). Ss then circle every third word. • Ss then write the mystery message in the spaces.

8A An evening at the Odeon

Aims: To practice adjectives of emotion

Instructions: Ex 1 • Give each S a photocopy of the worksheet. • Read the first sentence and example answer to the Ss, and show them how to complete the adjectives. • Ask Ss to suggest adjectives to complete the first movie review (*lonely, frightened, terrified*). • Ss complete the remaining reviews with the appropriate adjectives.

Ex 2 • Ss match the reviews to the posters.

8B New life

Aims: To practice *used to*, *be used to*, and *get used to*

Instructions: Ex 1 • Give each S a photocopy of the worksheet. • Read the first paragraph of the e-mail and draw the Ss' attention to the example answer 1. • Elicit which structure to use for number 2 (*get used to*). Ss write the answer in the space. • Ss complete the rest of the e-mail.

Ex 2 • Ss use the completed e-mail from Ex 1 to answer the comprehension questions.

Ex 3 • Ss write the highlighted letters from Ex 2 in the spaces. Then they reorder the letters to discover where Jack is.

8C Jimmy's bad week

Aims: To practice phrasal verbs with *in*

Instructions: Ex 1 • Give each S a photocopy of the worksheet. • Draw Ss' attention to the blog entries for each day, and read the first entry with the example answer. • Read the second entry and elicit the correct phrasal verb (*fit in*). • Ss complete the remaining entries with the phrasal verbs from the box.

Ex 2 • Read the first sentence again, and ask Ss to choose which picture it corresponds to. • Point out the example answer "Monday" under picture c). • Ss work in pairs to match the pictures to the sentences and write the day under the pictures.

Ex 3 • Ss work in pairs to discuss what the present could be. • Ss share their ideas with the class.

8D Consolidation 1 The sinking of the Titanic

Aims: To review *so + adjective/adverb, such a + noun*

Instructions: • Make a photocopy of the worksheet for each pair of Ss. • Cut the worksheets in half along the dotted line. • Arrange the Ss in pairs, Student A and Student B. • Give each student the Student A or Student B section of the worksheet.

Ex 1 • Show Ss that there is information about the sinking of the Titanic on the worksheets. • Draw Ss' attention to example answer 1. Explain that they need to complete the numbered spaces with *so* or *such*. Ss work in A pairs or B pairs to complete the exercise. • Explain that they don't need to fill in the information in the boxes at this stage.

Ex 2 • Reorganize the class, if necessary, into A/B pairs. • Ask the first question for Ss A "When did the Titanic set off?" and ask a Student B to answer (*April 10, 1912*). Show Ss B where to write the answer. • Then ask the first question for Ss B "Where did the Titanic set off from?" and ask a

Student A to answer (*Southampton*). Show Ss A where to write the answer. • Ss take turns asking and answering the questions and writing the information on their worksheets. • Ss compare their completed worksheets to check their answers.

> **Answer key: Ex 1** 1 so 2 so 3 such 4 so 5 so 6 so
> 7 so 8 such 9 so

8D Consolidation 2 Such a happy couple!

Aims: To review *so + adjective/adverb, such a + noun*

Instructions: Ex 1 • Give each S a photocopy of the worksheet. • Look at the cartoon story. Draw Ss' attention to the example answer in Frame 1. • Ss complete the conversation using the phrases in the box. • Read the completed conversation as a class.

Ex 2 • Draw Ss' attention to the final frame. Ask them to identify the four people. • Ask "How is Jack feeling?" (happy), and "Why?" and "How is Dora feeling?" (shocked, angry, worried), and "Why?" • Ss use their imaginations to complete Jack's sentence.

> **Answer key: Ex 1** 1 so upset 2 so selfish 3 so nice
> 4 such a beautiful 5 so tired 6 so much
> 7 so lazy 8 so quickly 9 such a great 10 so much time
> 11 so happy 12 so lucky
> **Ex 2** suggested answer: "such a wonderful/fantastic/great/enjoyable", etc.

9A What did she have done?

Aims: To practice causative *have*

Instructions: Ex 1 • Give each S a photocopy of the worksheet. • Draw Ss' attention to the receipts and notes. Elicit from Ss where Sarah went first (to the mechanic). • Look at sentence 1 with the example answer, and point out that it refers to the handwritten note "Car to mechanic". • Ss work in pairs to read and match the remaining sentences to the receipts and notes. • Read example sentence 1 again, and remind Ss of how to use

causative *have*. • Ss complete the sentences with the nouns/verbs in parentheses. Explain that they may need to use different tenses.

Ex 2 • Indicate the times on each receipt and note. • Ss work in pairs to figure out logically where Sarah went *before* having her car washed.

Ex 3 • Ss use the time information on the receipts and notes and the answer to Ex 2 to trace Sarah's route on the map.

> **Answer key: Ex 1** 1 c have her car repaired 2 f had her documents photocopied 3 a was having her hair cut 4 b have her teeth cleaned and polished 5 d had her photos printed 6 e had had her car washed
> **Ex 2** She must have returned to the mechanic to pick up her car before having it washed!
> **Ex 3** From Sarah's house – mechanic – copy shop – hairdresser – dentist – camera store – mechanic – carwash

9B Suffixes crossword

Aims: To review adjective suffixes

Instructions: Ex 1 • Give each S a photocopy of the worksheet. • Draw Ss' attention to the clue for 2 across and ask them to locate 2 across on the crossword. • Establish the number of letters (10), and ask Ss for the adjective that corresponds to the noun "mystery" (*mysterious*). • Ss write the correct answer in the crossword. • Ss complete the rest of the crossword.

Ex 2 • Ss use adjectives from the crossword or nouns from the clues to complete the names of the famous movies.

> **Answer key: Ex 1** Across: 2 mysterious 3 suspicious
> 7 beautiful 8 useful 9 attractive 11 ambitious
> 13 sunny 14 original 15 humorous
> Down: 1 dangerous 2 musical 4 imaginative 5 salty
> 6 effective 10 thirsty 12 wonderful
> **Ex 2** 1 Mystery 2 Wonderful 3 Dangerous 4 Beauty
> 5 Sun

9C The birthday present

Aims: To practice adjectives of texture and shape

Instructions: Ex 1 • Give each S a photocopy of the worksheet. • Look at the first picture and draw Ss' attention to the three adjectives. • Ask the Ss' why "slippery" is the word that doesn't belong (it can't be used to describe the toy). • Ss circle the adjectives that don't belong for the rest of the pictures.

Ex 2 • Draw Ss' attention to the example answer (slippery). • Point out that the numbers correspond to a letter, which they then write in the code grid. • Tell Ss to write s in all the boxes with the number 1. Ss transfer the adjectives from Ex 1 to the boxes and complete the code grid.

Ex 3 • Ss use the code grid to discover what Ellis got for his birthday.

Answer key: Ex 1&2 Words that don't belong are:
a) slippery b) smooth c) round d) rough e) oblong
f) straight g) rectangular h) fluffy

1	2	3	4	5	6	7	8	9	10	11	12	13	14	15	16	17	18	19
S	R	O	T	L	I	P	E	Y	M	H	U	G	B	N	A	C	D	F

Ex 3 football

9D Consolidation 1 Visitors' York

Aims: To review *look, seem, sound, feel, taste, smell* + adjective, */like/as if*

Instructions: Ex 1 • Give each S a photocopy of the worksheet. • Look at description 1, and draw Ss' attention to the example answer. • Read the next sentence, and elicit which phrase goes in the space (*feel as if*). Ss write the answer in the space. • Ss complete the remaining descriptions. Point out that each description has its own box of phrases to choose from.

Ex 2 • Ss read the full descriptions and match them to the photos.

Answer key: Ex 1 1 isn't like 2 feel as if 3 it seems as if 4 smells terrible 5 look and sound 6 feel like you've 7 looks beautiful 8 feels warm 9 smells delicious 10 looked like 11 tasted awful 12 seem very busy 13 felt as if 14 seemed so 15 sounds interesting 16 seems very busy 17 feel like you can't 18 seem expensive 19 look and taste 20 feel like
Ex 2 A Description 3 B Description 1 C Description 2

9D Consolidation 2 Something wrong

Aims: To review describing and dealing with problems

Instructions: • Make a photocopy of the worksheet for each pair of Ss. • Cut the worksheets in half along the dotted line. • Arrange Ss in pairs, Student A and Student B. • Give each student the Student A or Student B section of the worksheet.

Ex 1 • Draw Student A's attention to the first picture, and Ss B to the alternative solutions on their worksheets. • Ask a Student A to explain their problem and ask for help. • Ask a Student B to refuse the request, but offer an alternative solution. • Build the conversation on the board, if necessary.

Ex 2 • Ss change roles and repeat the procedure for Ex 1. • Ss then take turns to role-play the remaining situations on their worksheets.

10A An important appointment

Aims: To practice *should have/ought to have*

Instructions: Ex 1 • Give each S a copy of the worksheet. • Draw Ss' attention to the picture story. • Indicate the sentences and the verbs in the box. • Elicit which verb should go in the first sentence (*wear*), and show Ss the example answer (*should have worn*). • Ss complete all the sentences in the same way, using the correct form of the verbs.

Ex 2 • Draw Ss' attention to Frame f and the example answer (*1*). • The Ss then match the remaining sentences to each of the pictures.

Ex 3 • The Ss complete the speech bubble in the final frame.

Answer key: Ex 1 1 should/ought to have worn 2 should/ought to have taken 3 shouldn't have eaten 4 should/ought to have set 5 shouldn't have gone 6 shouldn't have left 7 should/ought to have brought 8 should/ought to have made
Ex 2 a 4 b 3 c 8 d 2 e 5 f 1 g 7 h 6
Ex 3 gotten married

10B Modern mysteries

Aims: To practice phrasal verbs with *away*

Instructions: Ex 1 • Give each S a copy of the worksheet. • Draw Ss' attention to the first article and the phrasal verbs in bold. • Read the first three sentences of the article together, and stop at the example answer for 1 (*looked away*). • Ask the Ss to scan the other phrasal verbs (in both articles) and suggest which is the correct answer for 2 (*ran away*). • Ss continue reading both articles and write the correct phrasal verbs in the spaces.

Ex 2 • Ask Ss to reread both completed articles. • Elicit the answer to question 1 (*Central Park*), and ask Ss to write the answer in the spaces. • Ss answer the remaining questions.

Ex 3 • Indicate the boxed letters in Ex 2. • Ss rearrange the letters to find the explanation for the mysteries.

Answer key: Ex 1 1 looked away 2 ran away 3 went away 4 threw away 5 passed away 6 gave away 7 put away 8 got away
Ex 2 1 Central Park 2 green 3 trash 4 twenty 5 Texas 6 note
Ex 3 hoaxes

10C The suspect

Aims: To review and practice vocabulary for crime

Instructions: Ex 1 • Give each S a photocopy of the worksheet. • Draw Ss' attention to the circled example (*suspect*), and ask what the other three words have in common (they are all verbs referring to crimes). • Ss work in pairs to identify and circle the word that doesn't belong in each group. • Check answers with the whole class, and encourage Ss to justify their answers.

Ex 2 • Ss write the circled words from Ex 1 in the box. • Ss then use the words in the box to complete the police interview.

Answer key: Ex 1 1 suspect 2 charge 3 vandalized 4 vandal 5 police officer 6 prison 7 deny 8 arrested
Ex 2 1 deny 2 vandal 3 police officer 4 arrested 5 vandalized 6 prison 7 suspect 8 charge

10D Consolidation 1 Excuses, excuses, excuses!

Aims: To review and practice language for apologizing

Instructions: • Make a photocopy of the worksheet for each pair of Ss. • Cut the worksheets in half along the dotted line. • Arrange the Ss in pairs, Student A, and Student B. • Give each S the Student A or Student B section of the worksheet.

Ex 1 • Draw Ss As' attention to their first situation, and Ss Bs' attention to their first picture. • Ask a Student A to read their situation and to express it as a complaint. • Ask a Student B to describe their excuse and to express it as an apology. • If necessary, use the board to build the conversation. • Ss role-play the three situations.

Ex 2 • Ss change roles and repeat the procedure for Ex 1.

10D Consolidation 2 Criminal pasts

Aims: To review vocabulary for crime

Instructions: • Give each S a photocopy of the worksheet. • Draw the Ss' attention to the picture, and explain that they have to discover the crime of each criminal and the sentence they received. • Read the clue *Pete admitted that he hadn't paid for a box of chocolates he got at the supermarket*, and elicit from Ss what crime he committed (*shoplifting*). • Ss write *shoplifting* in the correct place in the table. • Ss work in pairs, read the clues, and work out the crimes and sentences.

Answer key: 1 Pete: shoplifting, $2,000 fine 2 Alec: pickpocket, one year in prison 3 Ron: (bank) robbery, 15 years in prison 4 Jake: burglary, five years in prison 5 Max: vandalism, $800 fine

11A Here is the news

Aims: To practice vocabulary for the media

Instructions: Ex 1 • Give each S a photocopy of the worksheet. • Draw Ss' attention to the first anagram in the article and the example answer (*Newspapers*). • Ss rearrange the letters to find the rest of the "media" vocabulary and complete the article.

Ex 2 • Draw Ss' attention to the example answer. • Ss then write the rest of the answers from Ex 1 in the spaces.

Ex 3 • Ss write the highlighted letters from Ex 2 according to their numbers. • Ss then rearrange the letters to find the least popular people in the media.

11B Have your say!

Aims: To practice the language for giving opinions, agreeing, and disagreeing

Instructions: Ex 1 • Give each S a photocopy of the worksheet. • Ask Ss to read the three opinions from an Internet discussion site.

Ex 2 • Draw Ss' attention to the responses, and explain that there are three responses for each opinion, in columns A, B, and C. • Indicate the example response 1 (*that's a great*). • Ss complete the responses with the words and phrases from the box.

Ex 3 • Draw Ss' attention to response 1 in Column A again, and ask them which opinion it responds to. Point out the example answer (*1*). • Ss then match the rest of the responses to the opinions.

Ex 4 • Reread opinion 1 from Ex 1. • Elicit from Ss which of the three responses (1, 5, or 8) is closest to their personal opinion about downloading music. • Ss choose the A, B, or C answer that most closely matches their view for each opinion. • Ss count the As, Bs, and Cs and read their result.

11C Noun and adjective crossword

Aims: To practice adjective and noun formation

Instructions: Ex 1 • Give each S a photocopy of the worksheet. • Draw Ss' attention to the clue for 1 Across, and ask them to locate 1 Across on the crossword. • Point out the number of letters (ten), and ask Ss for the corresponding noun for the adjective "confident" (*confidence*). • Point out that the Down clues are nouns, and Ss have to write the adjectives. • Ss complete the rest of the crossword.

Ex 2 Ss put the highlighted letters from the crossword in the boxes to complete the proverb.

11D Consolidation 1 The best of British

Aims: To review mixed passive forms and practice asking questions in mixed passive forms

Instructions: • Make a photocopy of the worksheet for each pair of Ss. • Cut the worksheets in half along the dotted line. • Arrange Ss in pairs, Student A and Student B. • Give each S a Student A or a Student B section of the worksheet. • Show the Ss that there is information about the Mini on the worksheets.
• Ask the first question for Student A, using the cue *when?* (*When was the first Mini produced?*) and ask a Student B to answer it (*August 26, 1959*). Show Ss the example answer on the worksheet.

- Ask the first question for Student B, using the cue *who*? (*Who was it designed by?*) and ask a Student A to answer it (*Sir Alec Issigonis*). Show Ss the example answer on the worksheet. • Draw Ss' attention to the numbering sequence, then Ss ask each other the questions and complete the texts. • When they have finished, Ss compare texts to check.

11D Consolidation 2 Motivator quiz: the United States of America

Aims: To review mixed passive forms

Instructions: Give each S a photocopy of the worksheet. • Ss answer the quiz questions individually. • Check answers with the whole class. • Ss count up their total and read their result.

> **Answer key:** 1 c) more than 14 million
> 2 c) New Orleans 3 b) the World Trade Center
> 4 b) four times (St Louis 1904, Los Angeles 1932 and 1984, Atlanta 1996) 5 c) turkey 6 a) Central Park
> 7 c) San Francisco 8 b) John F. Kennedy 9 a) Jack Nicholson (twelve nominations, three wins; De Niro: six nominations, two wins; Hoffman: seven nominations, two wins) 10 c) Arnold Schwarzenegger

12A Money, money, money!

Aims: To practice verbs connected with money

Instructions: Ex 1 • Give each S a photocopy of the worksheet. • Read the first two sentences about Mike, and draw Ss' attention to the example answer (*spent*). • Elicit the verb for number 2 (*invest*) and ask the Ss which tense it should be. Ss write the answer in the space (*invested*). • Encourage Ss to read the full sentences before they choose the missing verbs. • Ss read and complete the three descriptions.

Ex 2 • Reread the first two sentences about Mike and ask Ss to figure out how much money he now has (*$11,000*). • Ss read the rest of the Mike description and calculate how much money he has at the end. • Check the answer (*$11,000*). • Ss work out how much money Dave and Jim have.

> **Answer key: Ex 1** 1 spent 2 invested 3 inherited
> 4 donated 5 splurged 6 earns 7 has saved
> 8 made 9 repay 10 lent 11 spent 12 invested
> 13 went 14 lost 15 owed 16 hadn't borrowed
> 17 repay 18 would have gone 19 won 20 paid
> **Ex 2** Mike has $11,000 Dave has $13,500 (after Jim has paid him back) Jim has $47,000

12B Pete and Olivia's world trip

Aims: To practice *wish/if only* + past perfect

Instructions: Ex 1 • Give each S a copy of the worksheet. • Draw Ss' attention to the picture story, and ask them to read what Olivia says in each frame. • Indicate the thought bubbles in each frame, and explain that these are Pete's thoughts. • Show Ss the completed thought bubble with the example answer (*'d used*). • Ss complete all the thought bubbles with the verbs, using the correct structures.

Ex 2 • Draw Ss' attention to the final frame. • Ask Ss where Olivia and Pete are now (*at home*), how they think Pete feels (*happy*), and how Olivia feels (*unhappy*). • Ss complete the sentence. • Let Ss compare their sentences with a partner or with the class.

> **Answer key: Ex 1** 1 'd worn 2 'd taken 3 hadn't ordered 4 'd used 5 'd stayed 6 'd learned
> **Ex 2** Possible answers: "I wish I was still in Hawaii!", "I wish I'd stayed in Hawaii!", "I wish I'd left Pete in Hawaii.", etc.

12C Congratulations!

Aims: To practice the language for giving and accepting congratulations

Instructions: Ex 1 • Give each S a photocopy of the worksheet. • Read the first conversation, and draw Ss' attention to the example answer (*Believe*). • Ask Ss to choose a word from the box for number 2 (*Great*). • Ss read and complete the three conversations.

Ex 2 • Ask Ss to match the conversations to pictures A, B, and C.

Ex 3 • Draw Ss' attention to example box 1, and establish that it is the beginning of a letter. • Ask Ss to identify which piece of the letter follows (*Just a*). Ss write 2 in the box. • Ss then number the rest of the pieces in the correct order. • Show Ss where to write the correctly ordered letter. • Refer Ss back to the three conversations, and ask them to identify who the letter is to. • Ss write the name of the person at the beginning of the letter.

> **Answer key: Ex 1** 1 Believe 2 Great 3 fantastic
> 4 never 5 can't 6 thrilled 7 must 8 day 9 Guess
> 10 deserve 11 have 12 true
> **Ex 2** Picture A: conversation 3   Picture B: conversation 2
> Picture C: conversation 1
> **Ex 3** Dear Matt, Just a quick note to say
> congratulations. I knew you could do it. You studied so
> hard. Good luck. I'm sure you'll do well. Best wishes
> from . . .

12D Consolidation 1 A life-changing decision

Aims: To practice *if* clause + past perfect

Instructions: Ex 1 • Give each S a photocopy of the worksheet. • Ask two Ss to read the first two parts of the conversation (up to "at the bank"). • Draw their attention to the example answers, and ask them what tense the sentence is in (*if* clause + past perfect).
• Ss use the *if* clause + past perfect to complete the rest of the conversation.

Ex 2 • Ask Ss to read through the completed conversation. • Read question 1, and ask Ss for the answer (*Manhattan*). Show Ss where to write the answer. • Ss answer the questions and write the answer in the spaces.

Ex 3 • Draw Ss' attention to the highlighted letters in Ex 2. • Ask Ss to rearrange the letters to create an ordinal number (*third*). • Point out that *top* is the third word. • Ask Ss to find the next third word (*model*) and write it in the space after *top*. • Ss circle every third word and complete the mystery fact.

> **Answer key: Ex 1** 1 hadn't gone 2 would still have
> been 3 wouldn't have stayed 4 it hadn't been
> 5 hadn't gotten 6 wouldn't have forgotten 7 hadn't
> been 8 wouldn't have lost 9 hadn't taken 10 wouldn't
> have been able 11 wouldn't have done 12 hadn't
> heard 13 wouldn't have offered
> **Ex 2** 1 Manhattan 2 karaoke 3 Frank Sinatra
> 4 record producer
> **Ex 3** third
> Top model Naomi Campbell was discovered while she
> was shopping in London.

12D Consolidation 2 Conversation crossword

Aims: To review the language for giving and accepting congratulations, verbs connected with money, and phrasal verbs with *out*

Instructions: • Give each S a copy of the worksheet. • Draw Ss' attention to the first line of Conversation 1, the example answer (*Guess*), and the text in parentheses at the end. • Explain that the number at the end refers to the number of letters in the answer. • Ss read the two conversations and complete the rest of the crossword.

> **Answer key:** Across: 1 guess 4 lucky 8 donate
> 10 found 11 afford 12 splurge
> Down: 1 Believe 3 eat out 5 borrowed 6 happen
> 7 celebrate 9 throw